A
GUIDEBOOK
TO
INTELLECTUAL PROPERTY

PATENTS, TRADE MARKS,
COPYRIGHT AND DESIGNS

AUSTRALIA
The Law Book Company
Brisbane • Sydney • Melbourne • Perth

CANADA
Carswell
Ottawa • Toronto • Calgary • Montreal • Vancouver

AGENTS
Steimatzky's Agency Ltd., Tel Aviv;
N.M. Tripathi (Private) Ltd., Bombay;
Eastern Law House (Private) Ltd., Calcutta;
M.P.P. House, Bangalore;
Universal Book Traders, Delhi;
Aditya Books, Delhi;
MacMillan Shuppan KK, Tokyo;
Pakistan Law House, Karachi, Lahore

A
GUIDEBOOK
TO
INTELLECTUAL PROPERTY

PATENTS, TRADE MARKS
COPYRIGHT AND DESIGNS

Fourth Edition

By

Robin Jacob Q.C.

and

Daniel Alexander

Barrister

LONDON · SWEET & MAXWELL · 1993

First Edition 1970
Second Edition 1978
Third Edition 1986
Fourth Edition 1993

Published by
Sweet & Maxwell Limited of
South Quay Plaza
183 Marsh Wall
London E14 9FT

Typeset by Tradespools Ltd.
Printed in England by Clays Ltd., St. Ives plc

A CIP catalogue record
for this book is available
for the British Library

ISBN 0 421 48730 5

No natural forests were destroyed to make this product
only farmed timber was used and re-planted

The index was prepared by Jenny Bough

The Authors' Right to be Identified has been asserted
in accordance with the Copyright, Designs and Patents Act 1988

PREFACE

This is the fourth edition of a book which started life as a series of pamphlets. In our chambers it is affectionately known as "Blanco's little book." You will find that it is rather different in approach to most of the other available books on intellectual property law.

It has two main aims. The first is to give the reader an overview and a feel for the subject. Since this is often lost in the morass of statutes and cases, we have deliberately kept our citations to a minimum.

The second is to provide a quick read for people (including, perhaps especially non-lawyers) who do not want to be too bothered with too much detail. Overall, the idea is to provide a book which can be read in one sitting, only dozing off once.

Because of this we have had to leave some things out. For example, those who are looking to find out precisely when copyright expires in particular kinds of work will have to look elsewhere. Those who want a detailed discussion on precisely what constitutes an "enabling disclosure" in patent law will be disappointed. Indeed, even those who want extensive statutory and case references for the relevant propositions, will recoil. Others still may be appalled at the absence of footnotes.

We make no apologies to such readers. There are many other very good books available containing more detail and analysis—we recommend some at the end. There are also many other books which are graver in tone. We have tried to preserve the inimitable (and some may say unorthodox) style and approach of the original author, Thomas Blanco White Q.C., formerly the head of our chambers to whom we dedicate this revision.

Robin Jacob
Daniel Alexander
The Temple, March 1993

CONTENTS

TABLE OF CASES

PART I

INTRODUCTION

1

IMITATION, MONOPOLY AND CONTROL

THE subject of this book is the law of commercial and industrial monopoly and imitation: imitation by one manufacturer of another's products, imitation by one trader of the names and badges by which another's goods or business are known. It is about how the law deals with the appropriation of the fruits of other people's labour. And it is also about how people can acquire monopoly rights to do certain profitable things (such as make certain products or sell them under particular names) and how those monopolies are protected and kept from getting out of hand. Thirdly, it is about how people can keep control over the use other people make of their creative work. These three subjects overlap to the point of inseparability in much of what follows.

The kinds of imitation

In law the means by which people acquire protection from imitation are best treated as distinct although in practice the kinds of imitation often overlap. There are numerous examples of such overlap. The manufacture of a particular industrial item might infringe a rival manufacturer's patent and also have been made by copying the rival's drawings (directly or indirectly). For another example, industrial designs are given protection in theory to protect the work of the designer—to protect the artistic element in manufacture. In many cases, however, the main value of design protection is to supplement the manufacturer's trade marks by securing to him exclusive rights in the "get-up" of the goods—a function that in legal theory belongs rather to the law of passing-off. For a third example, patent protection can be used in such a way as to build up the reputation of a trade mark for the patented goods such that the effect of the monopoly that the patent gave can be felt long after the patent has expired because the trade mark has by then become so well established. Exactly how to go about using, reinforcing and challenging the various monopoly rights to best commercial advantage is a matter for complex strategic assessment. Quite often it is possible to do almost as much with an unchallenged monopoly (such as a subsisting patent) as with one that is

3

secure (such as a *valid* subsisting patent) because the costs for a competitor of breaking the monopoly by legal action are often very high. The mere possession of a patent, however rubbishy to a lawyer's mind may be of real value for commercial purposes and it will encourage others to think of ways of "engineering round" the monopoly rather than face an action for infringement, once substantial resources have been committed. Because of the substantial costs for people of finding out exactly what it is they can do by getting a judge to tell them, a great deal of intellectual property law in practice involves not squabbling in court over the existence of rights but getting into the best position for reaching agreement on who should to be allowed to do what.

"Exclusive rights"

Most of the legal rights with which this book is concerned are rights to stop other people doing things. For some reason, Acts of Parliament do not put it like that: thus the proprietor of a registered industrial design is said by the Act to have "the exclusive right" to do certain things with the design, and the other rights are expressed in similar language. But what is meant is, not that the owner of the design, or patent, or copyright concerned has, by that ownership, the right to do anything he could not otherwise do, but that he has the right—subject to questions of validity—to decide whether other people shall be permitted to do certain things or not. This point is worth emphasising, because the position is too often not understood. In particular, many if not most of the people who take the trouble to secure patents for inventions believe that, somehow, possession of the patent secures to them the right to manufacture their inventions without interference. It does nothing of the sort: the thing such an inventor wants to manufacture may well incorporate other people's patented inventions, and the only way the inventor can be sure that he or she has the right to manufacture is by searching to find what patents other people have. His or her own patent (if it is valid, and the specification is properly drawn up—points discussed later in this book) confers the right to stop other people using the particular device that is the subject of the patent—and nothing else. In principle, the position is much the same with the other rights considered in this book, although ownership of a registered trade mark or service mark, exceptionally, gives a limited freedom from infringement of other people's marks.

Other rights

This book also deals with certain rights which are rather different from the above described rights to stop infringement: in particular it deals with forms of passing-off and the like which are different in nature; and it deals also with certain other parts of the law—such as the prevention of the misuse of confidential information and the action to prevent threats of patent litigation. By and large, what is said below about litigation applies in these cases too, although prosecutions to prevent and punish the use of false trade descriptions are different because such use is criminal in nature.

REMEDIES

Spatial and temporal monopolies

Intellectual property law gives people exclusive rights to do certain things (usually by way of exploiting particular markets for goods or services) in particular places and for specified times. The fact that the exclusive rights are limited by space and time causes a whole series of problems of international and particularly EEC law. For example: two of the key objectives of the Common Market are firstly to achieve free movement of goods and services by reducing the commercial importance of national boundaries and secondly to ensure that healthy competition takes place in the EEC. Both objectives stand in opposition to the structure of intellectual property law which firstly carves up the EEC by national boundaries (the scope and the length of patent protection, for example, is not the same in every Member State) and secondly gives people *monopoly* rights to de certain things. So one of the most practically important sources of law in recent years in this area has been decisions of the European Court of Justice and legislation from the European institutions. It is often these which determine how the subject matter of intellectual property law is exploited and traded.

The scheme of this book

This book is divided into sections broadly along the lines drawn by the main Acts of Parliament dealing with these branches of the law. The basic division is into three parts: the first part is concerned with the copying of the product and deals mainly with the law of patents and of industrial designs (for which there is a special registration system); the second part is concerned with the way things are sold and deals mainly with the law of passing-off, trade and service marks and other rules preventing unfair competition or unfair selling techniques; and the third part deals with the law of copyright (apart from its use to protect industrial designs) and certain related issues such as performance rights and "moral" rights. It also deals with the law of confidential information. The Copyright Act 1956 was the dominant statute on copyright for over a quarter of a century. On August 1, 1989 the key provisions of the Copyright, Designs and Patents Act 1988 came into force which made some important changes, principally in the law of copyright and industrial design. This book considers the new legislation and how it overlaps with the old.

It should be clear that this division into three sections is merely a matter of convenience. Commercial strategies and disputes often cut across these lines. It is one of the functions of this book to show the inter-relations between the different subjects in a way that more specialised works cannot easily do. There is a large amount of academic writing, some of it by lawyers and some by economists, on the value of particular intellectual property rights and the ways in which they are protected. For example, doubts are often expressed by industrialists about the value of patents at protecting the competitive advantage that their scientific innovations produce, and many companies now prefer to keep their inventions secret rather than disclose the details to the world, albeit in exchange for a limited monopoly. Often these concerns are industry specific, depending in part on how fast innovation occurs and can be commercially exploited. So a form of protection that might suit the chemical industry might be useless for heavy engineering. For another example, doubts are also often expressed by economists and industry analysts concerning the importance of the intellectual property system in providing incentives to research and innovate. The importance of providing proper incentives is one of the (several) justifications most frequently offered for giving people intellectual property rights in the first place. As with most Parliamentary output affecting industry, the legislation which is the source of most of the law with which this book deals is a mish-mash of compromise, some of it the result of effective lobbying by particular interest groups. There is not space in a book of this kind, which is devoted to describing how the system works, to give those arguments or the empirical work which has been done to support them, any detailed consideration.

Infringement

Since most of the various rights here discussed are similar in nature, they are enforced in essentially the same way—by an action in the courts (in England, normally in the High Court) for "infringement" of the right. The real point of most such actions is, that in this country, once the owner of the right has made it clear that he or she insists on it and once the court has declared that the right exists, few reputable business people will want to argue the point any further. Although the owner of the right usually asks for, and usually gets (if victorious) an injunction against further infringement—a formal order, that is, from the court to the infringer, forbidding infringement for the future—it is the decision that really matters, not the formal order. Indeed, such an order is so rarely disobeyed in commercial cases (where the defendant is almost always a company) that no really effective method of dealing with real disobedience has ever been worked out. In practice the thing to do against individuals who are determined infringers is to sue not only any companies which are controlled by them which are infringing for the time being, but also the individuals themselves. This prevents these individuals from forming new companies for the purpose of infringing—disobedience of an injunction by an individual means, ultimately, imprisonment.

But, not all business people are reputable, and there are sorts of infringement that call for sterner measures: counterfeiting of goods and their labels, piracy of tape recordings and video tapes in particular. These call for a specialised approach, perhaps involving simultaneous use of civil actions and criminal prosecutions. The technical details of the war against this sort of infringement are outside the scope of the present book, but it should be noted that our civil courts have developed a sort of search-warrant for really bad cases.

When to sue

An action for infringement can be brought either when infringement has already started, or at an earlier stage, when infringement is threatened; in general, the law allows one whose rights are infringed to choose when to sue. If infringement has already taken place, a successful plaintiff will be entitled to damages for what has already occurred as well as an order for the future, and an order that any goods or materials whose use would infringe the claimed rights be delivered up or rendered innocuous. In many cases, instead of damages it is possible to claim the profits the infringer has made from the infringement. However, litigation is expensive, and although the losing party will be ordered to pay the winner's costs, the amount paid will fall well short of covering the bills the winner will have to pay. Even if damages are reckoned in with the costs the loser pays, there is seldom money to be made by this sort of litigation. Actions are often brought to punish the infringer, to stop further infringement by him or others and to establish the legal position for the future; very seldom are they brought for the sake of the damages. It follows that, in almost all cases, the right time to start an action for infringement (if an action is to be started at all) is when infringement first starts—or even better, when infringement is first threatened. This is especially true of actions for infringements of trade or service marks and of actions to stop passing-off, since in these cases the right to sue may be lost by delay.

There are other reasons why actions for infringement are best brought quickly if they are to be brought at all. The best way to win an action is not to have to fight it; so that the best sort of action to start is the sort that will not be defended. Whether an action is defended or not naturally depends in large degree on whether the case is important enough to the defendant to make it worth while going to the trouble and expense of fighting—and facing the uncertainty of not knowing what the result will be. The defendant in an infringement action faces the prospect of an injunction against continuing the offending business, and it is not easy to plan ahead not knowing whether such an injunction will be issued or not. Accordingly, just as few people start infringement actions unless they feel they must, so few people defend them unless they feel they must. If an infringer is allowed to infringe in peace for years—to spend money advertising a new business or a new product; to develop a new market to the point where it becomes profitable, perhaps even to build a new factory or re-equip an old one—there may be no real option but to fight; yet if the action had been brought earlier on, before there was so much at stake, the offending activity would probably have been dropped rather than waste time and money fighting. There are always other products and other markets. In trade mark cases especially is this so: it is very rarely worth fighting for a new mark, even if the chances are in your favour.

Time and cost

Although the various rights with which this book is concerned are all enforced by actions of much the same nature, the cost and complexity of litigation varies widely between the different cases. Actions for infringement of patent are in a class by themselves: in complexity, in cost, in the time needed to bring them to trial. Few patent disputes are finally settled within three years; so that an infringement which will have ceased to be commercially important within three years or so is often hardly worth suing over at all, whilst an infringer who can be sure of stopping infringement within three years or so can often face the possibility of an action with comparative equanimity. This considerably reduces the practical value of patents. A copyright, trade mark or passing-off action may be brought to trial in a matter of months, and the cost and trouble are much less, too. Actions for infringement of industrial designs are intermediate in character; whether they are more like patent actions or more like copyright actions depends on how the parties handle them.

Interlocutory injunctions

There are cases in which to wait a matter of months is to wait months too long. In these cases, the court may be asked to act at once, and to grant at the outset an injunction against infringement—not a permanent injunction, but an interlocutory one, lasting until the trial of the action. In particular, many trade or service mark infringements, many cases of passing-off (especially where there is a suggestion that the defendant is dishonest), and many infringements of copyright are best dealt with in this way. A plaintiff who is granted an interlocutory injunction must give what is called a "cross-undertaking in damages": that is, the plaintiff must undertake that, if in the end the action fails, he will compensate the defendant for the interference to the defendant's business effected by the injunction. In most cases, this is not an important matter; but an interlocutory injunction in a patent case may well stop a production line, and the damage caused to the defendant may be very great. At the same time, the final result of the action is seldom entirely certain. So the risk to the plaintiff involved in asking for an interlocutory injunction may be too great and should be carefully considered before an application for an interlocutory injunction is made. Provided the plaintiff acts as soon as the infringement is brought to light—this is essential—an interlocutory injunction will often be granted by the court in order to preserve the status quo until the trial. Unless the evidence fails to disclose that the plaintiff has any real prospect of success at the trial, the court will consider whether the balance of convenience lies in favour of granting or refusing an interlocutory injunction. An important consideration in weighing the balance of convenience is whether the plaintiff or the defendant will be adequately compensated in damages if an interlocutory injunction is either wrongfully refused or wrongfully granted. The court tries to make an order at the interlocutory stage which will put the trial judge in the best position of being able to do justice at the end of the day.

Inspection and discovery orders

In the last few years, cases of piracy have become much commoner in many different fields of commerce. Partly in response to this, the courts have held that in extreme cases, orders can be made upon the application of the plaintiff alone requiring the defendant to permit the plaintiff's solicitors to inspect his documents and premises immediately. They are called *Anton Piller* orders after one of the early cases in which one was granted. The purpose of this is of course that an unscrupulous defendant is given no time to destroy incriminating documents or evidence. The courts have also held that even innocent persons who have become "mixed up" in the wrongdoing (*e.g.* the Customs, or innocent warehousemen and the like) can be compelled to disclose at least the name of the wrongdoer. Such persons (save, possibly, the Customs who are in a special position) can also be restrained from permitting pirate goods from leaving their possession until at least there has been time for the case to come properly before the court. Defendants are protected against abuse of these "search warrants" by stringent conditions governing their grant. In recent years the courts have been much more careful to ensure that defendants are given proper protection.

FOREIGN LAW

This is a book about English law. Almost all foreign legal systems have something corresponding more or less to the various rights discussed in this book, but the correspondence is seldom close. Commonwealth countries, and to some extent the United States too, have legal systems like ours; but their patent law is our old patent law, not our new one (see Chap. 3) and few of them have our use of copyright to control copying of manufactured goods. Other countries, including European countries, have basically different legal systems, so that even where their law is supposed to be the same as ours—as with the new European patent law, see Chapter 3—it is unlikely to work out in practice the same way as ours.

NOTE: COMPENSATION FOR INFRINGEMENT

The usual procedure in any action for infringement is that the issue of liability is decided first: only if the plaintiff wins, does the issue of how much compensation the defendant must pay him arise. The successful plaintiff has then a choice: to be compensated according to the damage the infringement has done to his own business, or, instead, to have paid over to him the profits made by the infringer from the infringement. In either case, only the damage suffered or profits made in the six years immediately prior to the issue of the writ in the action and since the issue of the writ can be awarded. In exceptional cases, where the court for some reason disapproves of the plaintiff's conduct, profits can be refused, but damages can be refused only in special cases discussed below. Of course, neither problem may arise in some cases—for example where the infringer merely made samples of an infringing article to see what would happen.

What happens in practice is this: the plaintiff makes his choice of damages or profits and the courts orders a corresponding investigation. Before the investigation takes place (before, therefore, the plaintiff and defendant have seen each other's books) the infringer usually makes an offer (he may even have made this offer earlier, before the issue of liability was determined). If the plaintiff accepts, well and good; if the plaintiff refuses, the investigation takes place, but at the plaintiff's risk as to costs: if the amount found due is less than was offered the plaintiff pays for the investigation; if it is more the infringer pays. Normally, the infringer pays "into court" (into an official bank account) the amount offered.

(a) Damages

If the plaintiff elects to have damages the court orders an inquiry into just how and how much the infringement has injured the plaintiff. There is an exception to this, however, in the case of patents, designs and copyright where an infringer can escape the payment of damages if, at the time of the infringement, he was not aware, and had no reasonable grounds for supposing, that the monopoly infringed existed. (Such innocence is not uncommon in patent and design cases: it is rare in copyright cases, since most "works" of recent origin are pretty well bound to be copyright and the infringer who copies them ought to have known that. Note that in any case, the infringer who goes on infringing after warning can no longer be innocent.)

In copyright cases begun before August 1, 1989, the plaintiff could claim, additionally, damages not only for infringement but also for conversion: that is he could demand to be treated as the owner of all infringing copies of his work, and if the infringer or anyone else disposed of any or destroyed them then the plaintiff could claim damages for loss of his property, provided that this did not double compensate the plaintiff. These damages were widely considered to be unduly harsh and the right to claim conversion damages has been abolished by the Copyright, Designs and Patents Act 1988.

As to the measure of damages, the plaintiff is entitled to exact compensation for any monetary damage he has actually suffered that can be fairly attributed to the infringement. Thus, if an infringing book or machine has sales of so many, the author or inventor will have lost so many royalties. A plaintiff who is a manufacturer or publisher can ask the court to assume (unless the infringer can show that this was not so) that each infringing sale has cost him a sale, and so lost him the profit on a sale. There may be other heads too: the owner of a trade or service mark which is infringed may have to pay for additional advertising to restore the position; the owner of an infringed patent or design may be forced, whilst waiting for the action to be tried, to reduce profit margins in order to retain any share of the market. All that can go in. Or the matter may be approached in a different way: pirating of a copyright work may render the work valueless, or passing-off may partly or wholly destroy a goodwill. Damages may be assessed by estimating the value of the copyright before and after the infringement and taking the difference. Some cases are complicated of course; but it is seldom difficult to make a rough estimate of the sum likely to be involved. The key question, when dealing with a manufacturer-plaintiff, is: what is his profit on a sale?

In the case of particularly serious infringements of copyright, the court may award a plaintiff additional damages. Before the 1988 Act the court could only award such damages in very limited situations (where the plaintiff would otherwise be denied effective relief) but now the court has a general discretion to award additional damages. In deciding whether they are appropriate, particular regard must be had to the flagrancy of the infringement and any benefit accruing to the defendant by reason of the infringement. One example of a situation in which such damages might be awarded is where a journal publishes material believing that the profits (or enhancement of reputation) he would gain from publication would exceed the compensation which a plaintiff would be likely to recover.

(b) Profits

When it comes to taking an account of profits, it is the infringer's profits that matter, not the plaintiff's. They are harder to assess. For one thing, it is difficult to judge the extent to which (in assessing the profit from infringement) that particular part of the business can properly be loaded with overheads, or even promotion expenses. In addition it is the profits from infringement that matter, and they may or may not be separable from other matters giving rise to profits. Suppose, for example, a book of which only part infringes; or a stocking, of which all that was patented was the way the toe was made. It may be very difficult to say what part of the profit is attributable to that. It is often even harder for a plaintiff to guess what the answer is going to be before he has seen the defendant's books. Accordingly, it is usually too risky to ask for an account of profits and it is seldom asked for in practice. Not always, however. Suppose that the inventor of the stocking toe can say: "Making the toe my way saves, on average, per dozen pairs of stockings, so many minutes of operative's time at so much an hour"—then an estimate of the profit from the invention is directly available for comparison with estimates of damages before the plaintiff makes his election.

In copyright cases innocence is no defence to a claim for profits. In other cases it probably usually is a defence.

NOTE: SELF-HELP IN COPYRIGHT INFRINGEMENT

Since 1989 there has been a partial self-help remedy for copyright infringement only to be exercised with great caution. This is in addition to the inspection and discovery orders referred to above.

After notifying the local police station, a copyright owner can seize infringing copies which are found exposed or immediately available for sale (such as in a street market). Adequate notice must be left for the alleged infringer. An alternative, and safer route, is to apply to court for an order that the offending articles be delivered up.

NOTE: EXCLUSIVE LICENSEES

An exclusive licensee is someone who is given rights under a patent or copyright exercisable *to the exclusion of the right holder.* Exclusive licensees are given special rights to sue. In the case of copyright and patents, an exclusive licensee of a copyright or the patent has concurrent rights to sue and can pursue an action as if he or she were the copyright owner or patentee. There are certain formalities which must be observed in the case of exclusive patent licensees in order not to lose rights to damages.

Similarly a registered user of a registered trade mark can sue, but he or she must first call upon the proprietor to do so. If the proprietor does not take action within two months, the registered user can sue.

In each case, the proprietor of the right must be joined into the proceedings but the court can dispense with this requirement in the case of copyright.

2

PATENT, COPYRIGHT OR DESIGN?

IN considering protection of a new product against imitation, the first question is whether the case calls for patenting, can be left to copyright or design right or is one of the special cases where design registration is advisable.

PATENTS

A patent is granted to protect an article that is essentially better in some way than what was made before, or for a better way of making it. The monopoly a patent gives can extend to any other improved article or process which is better for the same reasons as that on which the patent is based. In an extreme case, a patent can be wide enough and represent a big enough advance over earlier ideas to give its owner a complete monopoly of an industry. For instance, there have been patents giving for a time a monopoly of telephones, a monopoly of pneumatic tyres or a monopoly of transistors. Very few patents are as important as that, but the existence of almost any patent (if it is, or is thought to be, valid) will make it necessary for a competitor to do design work or even major research of his own rather than copy the actual product he wishes to imitate.

When patents suffice

Whether in a particular case the law of patents can give a manufacturer the protection he needs, depends mainly on three things: how new his product is, how important it is, and for how long he needs protection. The degree of novelty will decide whether he can get a patent, and if so how wide a monopoly this patent may be made to give him. The importance of the product will decide how much trouble it will be worth a competitor's taking to get over the monopoly and how big a risk of legal attack a competitor will be prepared to face. The time factor may decide whether it is practicable to carry out the design or research work needed to avoid a monopoly whose validity cannot safely be challenged.

14

If, then, a manufacturer needs freedom from competition while he builds up a new business of substantial size, only a patent of unusually wide scope with a really important invention behind it will do: any ordinary patent could be got over by competitors long before the business was firmly established. If what is wanted is a monopoly in a new line of goods not of great importance a patent of comparatively narrow scope should suffice, for it will usually be less trouble for competitors to produce something different than to risk trouble with patents. In intermediate cases it may be very hard to get proper protection: where goods are markedly more successful than what was made before without being very strikingly different, it is doubtful whether any patent can prevent imitation. This point is important and will be considered more fully in the course of the next two chapters.

DESIGNS, REGISTERED AND UNREGISTERED

Unregistered design right

Unregistered design right is the appropriate means of protection for designs for industrial articles. Like copyright, it arises without the need for any special registration or application, so it is cheap to obtain. Also, like copyright, it does not give a complete monopoly, it only prevents copying, so if others come up with the same design independently they cannot be stopped.

Registration of designs

Registration of a design is none too cheap and must be done before the design is shown to anyone otherwise than in strictest confidence. But sometimes it should be worthwhile. In particular, the sort of design that someone else would be sure to come up with fairly soon may call for registration, to deal with competitors who reach the same design independently. A copyright is not infringed except by actual copying, but a registered design (if validly registered) is infringed by anyone using the same design even if he thought of it independently. Inevitably, though, it is much easier to persuade a court that someone else's design is the same as yours if you can show that he actually copied it.

Copyright

Copyright

Copyright is principally designed to protect literary, artistic, and musical works as well as other products of what may loosely be called the entertainment industry—films, sound recordings, broadcasts and the like. It arises automatically as soon as a work is physically recorded, without the need for any formalities, application or registration. (Some people think that to "copyright" a work you have to put a little "c" in a circle on it but this is not so.) Copyright had an important role to play in protecting industrial designs, but since the introduction of the unregistered design right, that has been much diminished.

Copyright gives a right to prevent copying. It does not give a complete monopoly in the sense that a patent does.

Computer software

Computer programs are, in general, copyright; and the copyright is infringed both when a listing of the program is copied (copied as a listing, or recorded as a runnable program) and when an object-code or assembly-code version is reproduced. Programming techniques, as distinct from actual programs, call for patent protection: they are not supposed to be patentable, but there are ways in which this can be done—so far, anyway.

PERIODS OF PROTECTION

The periods of protection given by patents, copyrights and design registrations are all different.

(a) Patents

A patent lasts—so long as renewal fees are paid—for 20 years from the date when the full specification of the invention is filed at the Patent Office (this need not be the date of first application for a patent). Patent protection, however, does not become fully effective until the specification is published by the Patent Office. This will take up to 18 months from the date when the patent is applied for. The patenting of a quickly-produced and short lived line of goods may thus be completely useless: the patent may have lost its importance before it comes fully into force.

Of course the delay in publication may sometimes be an advantage, for the invention can be kept secret until publication date.

(b) Copyright

Copyright in an artistic work arises when the work is made so that the owner of the copyright gets immediate protection and there is no period of waiting for registration. In general, the period of copyright is the life of the author plus 50 years, but there are many exceptions.

(c) Unregistered design right

Design right lasts for at most 15 years from the year in which the design was made. But it expires after ten years, if the design is first marketed within the first five years of the life of the design right. Also, five years after first marketing by the designer, it is possible to apply for compulsory licences.

(d) Registered designs

The registration procedure for a design may take about six months, and until then there is no registration and no protection. (So, with articles that are very quick and easy to copy, such as most things moulded in plastics, registration ought to be applied for some six months before they are first shown to the trade, and then copying can be stopped at once.) The registration lasts for five years from the application, and can be kept alive on payment of further fees for four further five-year periods. Few design owners find this worth doing.

"Imitations" and Copying

In an action for infringement of a patent or a design registration, it makes, in theory, no difference whether infringing goods are copied from those of the owner of the patent or design, or the makers of the infringements worked entirely on their own. In practice, a defendant who has copied is always more likely to lose the action; but in theory the only questions to be decided are first: whether the patent or design registration is a valid one; and, secondly, whether the monopoly given by it is wide enough to cover the alleged infringement. Even if the "infringer" did not know of the existence of the patent or registration concerned this will not make any difference to the giving of an injunction against him; nor even in most cases to his liability to pay damages and to pay the costs of the action. In an action based on copyright the position is different: the action will only succeed if it can be shown that the alleged infringement was copied (directly or indirectly) from the copyright work.

It follows that a new product, developed entirely by the staff of the company that makes it, may well be an infringement of patent or registered design rights belonging to a competitor. Throughout this book, when we speak of "imitations," we mean to include such independently developed products. In the case of registered designs, the risk is not usually very serious and can be easily avoided by a proper search. The risk of innocent infringement of patents, however, in any industry where there is appreciable technical progress, will usually be a serious one if the new product is noticeably different from the old. There is no way of avoiding this risk except thorough acquaintance with or thorough search of all existing patents in the branches of industry concerned; in fields such as electronics these may number thousands. No attempt is made in this book to suggest any other way, and discussions in later chapters on avoiding patents refer only to patents whose existence is already known. A thorough search of a field of any size is difficult and rather expensive; a good patent agent will do it as cheaply as it can be done.

The essence of a patent is that the inventor gets a monopoly in return for full disclosure of his invention in the specification which he files at the Patent Office and the Patent Office publishes. (These published specifications are an extremely valuable source of information in many fields; in some fields they are almost the only reliable source of information about recent developments.) Sometimes, however, technical knowledge is best protected by not publishing it at all. Even where an invention is patented, those who work it soon acquire special knowledge of how to work it. The law will sometimes protect such unpublished information. It is discussed in Chapter 22.

PART II

PROTECTING THE PRODUCT

3

PATENTS AND HOW TO GET THEM

THE SYSTEMS OF PATENT LAW

There are now two sorts of patent in force in this country: "old Act" patents (applied for before mid-1978) and "new patents" (applied for thereafter). Because the term of a patent is now 20 years, the last old Act patents will expire in mid-1998. The main difference between the two sorts of patent is that the grounds available for challenging validity of old Act patents are somewhat different from those available for new Act patents (see the note at the end of this Chapter).

The basis of the new system introduced in 1978 was harmonisation of the patent laws of different European (not only EC) countries. Until then each country had its own patent office and own independent laws. By the EPC (European Patent Convention) of 1973 the participating countries (now 16, not just EC countries) agreed to bring their own laws into conformity with the Convention and to set up a common system for granting patents. European countries then enacted new national patent laws and our own Patents Act 1977 was part of that process. No country was willing to give up its own patent office and so a compromise was reached. An inventor can apply for his patent either through a national patent application ("the national route") or through the EPC route. This latter route involves an application to the EPO ("European Patent Office") in Munich, the inventor choosing ("designating") the European countries in which he wants a patent and paying fees accordingly. Subject to one complication (so-called "oppositions"—see below) once a patent is granted by the EPO it takes effect in each designated country just as if it had been granted by that country's national patent office. We call a patent granted by this route a "European Patent (UK)" but it is not, as its name may suggest, really European. It is British patent with corresponding sister patents in other European countries.

There is one further procedure we should mention: the PCT ("Patent Co-operation Treaty"). This is procedural only: although an application made by this route is called an "international application" it in fact leads to parallel national patents in different countries. An application is made (so far as UK residents are concerned) to our own Patent Office. This checks formalities and then sends the application to the appropriate searching office for that type of invention (this will usually be a foreign office). If the applicant wants (he generally will), the searching office will reach preliminary conclusions on novelty and obviousness. Some countries' patent offices are apt to accept these. Thus the applicant is able to get a fairly early indication of how good his patent might be, and, if things do not look good, quit before he has spent too much money. If all is well the application is then passed to the patent offices of the countries where he wants patents and proceeds as ordinary applications there. The system is administered by WIPO ("World Intellectual Property Organisation," a UN agency) in Geneva. The procedure is complex (with some risk, therefore, of things going wrong) but patent agents have now got used to it and it is increasingly being used. Sometimes it has financial advantages: for instance it treats all the EPO countries as one, which saves fees at an early stage. They have to be paid later, of course, but then the application may never get that far. Most countries are now parties to the PCT.

More ambitious plans for the internationalisation of patent law exist, but are not yet in effect. For instance there is a plan for a single Common Market patent. Originally proposed in the Community Patent Convention of 1975, talks have been on and off for many years. There are real complications, for instance the question of a court to administer the law outside national systems of law and questions of national independence. Perhaps not surprisingly one of the countries unwilling to help get the system going has been Denmark. Tidy though the idea is in theory, in practice it will probably cost too much and will not bring about much more certainty. So industry does not seem to be pressing hard for it. Another plan under discussion in Geneva at WIPO is a world treaty for bringing the laws of different countries (principally the USA, Europe and Japan) more into line with each other.

What route, European or British?

Since he can get a patent here either via the EPO in Munich or via the British Patent Office (in Wales) an inventor can choose which system to use. Indeed he can, initially, choose both, though once the EPO grants a patent with the UK as a designated country, any British patent disappears. A number of factors will influence the inventor's choice of route. And he can possibly use the "international route" of the PCT rather than applying directly to the EPO or British Office.

First cost; there are a number of factors involved here. Obviously there are official fees. Official fees are not the only factor, however. If one uses the EPO one can use just one patent agent. Moreover there is no need in the EPO at an early stage for translations. The application can be filed in just one of the official languages (English, French or German) and the whole application proceeds in that language. Only later, when and if the patent is granted, is there need for translation into other European languages. If one uses the national route then translations are needed from the beginning of applications for protection abroad which will be, under the International Convention (mentioned in the next Chapter) a year from the initial application. Generally speaking, if a patent is wanted in more than three countries then the EPO is cheaper. Three countries is about break even. The following is a rough indication of cost (including a patent agent's fees) for an invention where there are few complications: initial draft of specification £750–1,500 (to be spent before any application); £5,000 to EPO grant and £1,500 per country. Patent agents have devised ingenious ways of delaying the time when fees need to be paid. This can be important, since it gives the inventor more time to see whether what he has got is important and whether his patent is likely to be any good.

Next speed; the British Office is markedly faster to grant than the EPO. For instance in the case of the genetically engineered product tpA (a blood de-clotter) both our High Court and Court of Appeal had heard the case (and held the invention obvious) within two-and-a-half years of grant by the British Office. The corresponding EPO application (made at the same time) was still pending a year later and is still under opposition in the EPO some five years after grant. The lesson is obvious: if you think you will need to enforce your monopoly soon, go British.

Thirdly, validity and scope; a patent drawn up to suit the practice of one country will seldom be fully suited to others. So international applications (for the whole world) or EPO applications which use a single specification for all countries may not be as good as individually tailored applications.

Fourthly, there is the "eggs in one basket" verses the "gap in protection" problem. If the inventor goes the European route and something goes wrong (*e.g.* the Office holds the patent invalid and an appeal fails) then he loses for all designated countries (unless he has also gone via national routes also). This is particularly important in relation to "oppositions" in the EPO—see below. On the other hand, if he goes only via national routes then, if the application fails in one country he will have a gap in his European protection. If he goes via both routes it will cost a lot more, but he will have the maximum flexibility and security against things going wrong, even though he will have to chose between the patent granted by the EPO and that granted by the British Office.

WHO APPLIES

The right to apply for a patent belongs to the owner of the invention—the inventor himself, or anyone who can claim the invention from him. Other people can join in the application.

Most inventions are made by employees, as part of their job: in such cases, the employer owns the invention (see Note at the end of this chapter) and can apply to patent it, although he needs the inventor's signature (unless the invention is a foreign one, and he is patenting it here under the International Convention mentioned below). Or the inventor can make the application (in which case he will be a sort of trustee of it for his employer); or they may both apply together (when the inventor will still be a sort of trustee of his half-share).

THE SPECIFICATION AND THE CLAIMS

The applicant must file at the Patent Office a document called a specification. This must contain a description of the apparatus or process or article, or whatever is to be the subject of the patent. It must contain instructions which will enable a skilled man to work the process, or make the apparatus or article as the case may be. Most important of all it must contain what are called "claims": that is, statements defining the precise scope of the rights of monopoly that the patent will give. There is only one way of finding out whether the owner of a patent can prevent the manufacture and sale of a particular imitation of his patented product, and that is by looking up his specification and seeing whether the words of the "claims" describe that imitation. Note that the form of the specification which matters is the "B" specification. This is the one with "B" after the patent number. The specification with an "A" after the number is the form as filed by the patentee. In other words the "A spec." is what he asked for, the "B spec." what he got. Claims are usually written in special jargon (to make them as generalised as possible) and a good deal of practice is needed to understand exactly what they are saying. Likewise a good deal of practice is needed to write them. The heart of a patent agent's craft lies in claim drafting.

Most patent disputes include an argument about the meaning (what the lawyers call "construction") of the claims. Generally the patentee says they are wide enough to cover the thing he is complaining about and the defendant denies it. Often the defendant adds that if they are wide enough to catch him they also cover something old or obvious and so are bad. We in Britain are reasonably careful about patent claims. After all they are there for telling people not only what they cannot do but also, by converse, what they can. And it is the patentee (or at least his patent agent) who draws the fence in the first place. Although foreign countries have claims in their patents and in theory might seem to use them as we do, this is seldom so in practice. Most European countries (parties to the EPC) are indeed supposed to treat claims in exactly the same way and there is a special "Protocol to Art. 69" which tries to achieve this. But all that says is that the claims should be construed in the context of the description and drawings (which we have always done anyway) and not used as a "guideline." In practice it seems that Continental countries still treat claims rather more liberally than we do, particularly in relation to so-called "equivalents." The Americans also have a more liberal doctrine here.

Two examples

The patent in *Catnic* v. *Hill & Smith*, 1982 was for a "box lintel"—a building component for going over doors or windows. Old lintels were made of reinforced concrete. The Catnic idea was to use a hollow steel box shaped appropriately. The patent claim called for two horizontal plates "substantially parallel" to each other and, in addition to an inclined support member, a "second rigid support member *extending vertically*" from one horizontal plate to the other. The row was over the meaning of "extending vertically." What the defendant did was to use a support member which was 6° off true vertical but which was good enough to work. He said that the claim meant true vertical—emphasising his point by contrasting the way the claim dealt with the horizontal plates. It was enough for these to be "substantially parallel" whereas the word "vertical" was not qualified. The House of Lords had no difficulty in dismissing this argument as a lawyer's quibble. A practical man would regard any member vertical enough to work as "vertical." The only wonder of the case is how the Court of Appeal ever thought otherwise.

On the other hand, in *Improver* v. *Remington*, 1989 the patent was for a device for removing hair from women's legs—in the refined language of the patent, a depilator. The patentee had the idea of using a helical spring bent in a curve. One end was fixed to a small high speed electric motor and the other to a fixed bearing. The spring rotated at high speed and its windings opened and closed rapidly, catching and pulling out the hairs. The patent claim called for a "helical spring." The wily defendant substituted for this a rubber rod with transverse slits. When this was rotated the slits opened and closed just as in the case of the windings of the helical spring. But, both here and in Hong Kong, the courts held there was no infringement. True it was that the rod had all the necessary properties of the helical spring (it was appropriately "bendy" and "slitty") but it was not a helical spring. To find infringement it would have been necessary to ignore the word "helical" altogether, or regard it as no more than a kind of shorthand for a component having the necessary properties.

Interestingly the corresponding German court took a different view, for in Germany there is, it seems, a doctrine of infringement by exact and obvious equivalents of items specified in a claim. Quite how that is reconciled with the requirement that the invention be specified in the claim we are not sure. There is a similar rule in the U.S. From the point of view of a student of comparative patent law (apart of course from the lawyers involved) it is a great pity that this case was not fought all over the world because its facts are easy to understand and the legal approaches of different countries would have been easy to study. From the point of view of a British lawyer or patent agent the case is an excellent example of the danger of being too specific in the widest patent claim. If it had said in Claim 1 "means for removal of hair" and by a Claim 2 "wherein said means is a helical spring" there would have been no difficulty. But then it is always easy to be wise after the event. Some good patent agents do favour the "means for" approach. It forces the patentee to think about the function of each item making up his invention.

SECURING PRIORITY

Preparation of a specification is usually a long job, and it is often important that the patent should be applied for at the earliest possible moment. But the Act allows the applicant to secure a right of priority by filing an informal application in the first place (here or abroad); he then has a year to prepare and make a proper application. So long as the invention is well enough described in the original application to "support" the claims of the final one, the novelty of his invention will be judged as of the earlier date. The original application can simply be dropped: but there are snags; see "Delay in application" below. If it is dropped, the only penalty for getting the original specification wrong is loss of priority. The specification of the application that is finally proceeded with, however, not only has to pass detailed scrutiny by expert examiners at the Patent Office but also must be proof against the destructive criticism of hostile lawyers and experts: for if the patent is ever the subject of legal proceedings, the wording of the specification may determine the validity and scope of the patent.

Just what is necessary for an earlier specification to "support" the claims of a later one is not clear; as usual in our present Patents Act, the draftsman has been careful not to use words that mean anything very definite, either to a lawyer or to anyone else.

PATENTABILITY

Not every bright idea is patentable. A patentable invention has to be "capable of industrial application"—including exploitation in agriculture, but excluding plant or animal varieties and "essentially biological processes for the production of animals or plants." Microbiological processes, though, can be patented; they are rather important, since many antibiotics are made by fermentation as well as many drinks. Medical and veterinary treatments are not patentable; but drugs are (even if the materials used are old; see Note to Chap. 5).

There is also a list of matters excluded from patentability as being essentially intellectual: scientific theories; mathematical methods; computer programs; aesthetic creations of all sorts. It used to be possible to "dress up" a claim to a computer program as some sort of device claim (a computer organised to run the program) but this has got harder. For instance a chip containing a novel and inventive program for finding square roots was held unpatentable, *Gale*, 1991. The EPO has evolved a test namely, is there a "technical effect" for patentability but it is not entirely clear what this means. Borderline cases in this area will always be improved by ingenious framing of claims, another reason why the services of an experienced patent agent can be so valuable. One area where controversy rages now is the patentability of genetically engineered animals (there is no problem over bacteria). The EPO is making up its mind slowly on the point. The EPO has decided in favour of patentability in this area, but there is strenuous opposition to this. The American office has decided in favour of patentability (in the "Harvard Mouse" case—a mouse which develops cancer so it can be used in cancer research) and probably the final decision will go that way in Europe too.

SEARCH, PUBLICATION, EXAMINATION

If it is intended to proceed with a patent application the next step is to request (and pay for) a preliminary examination and a search of earlier patents. The preliminary examination goes to the formal correctness of the application and specification; the search, in the first place at least, will be through earlier published British specifications for the same sort of invention. At the same time, the application and its specification will be published, probably 18 months after filing. This means that if the inventor wants to avoid publication (as he may: see below, under "Delay in application") the application must be withdrawn.

The next stage is for the applicant to request (and, as usual, pay for) a full examination. Here the examiner considers whether what is claimed is the sort of thing that is patentable at all; whether the specification is clear and complete enough to enable a skilled reader to work the invention; and above all, whether when compared with what appears in earlier specifications the invention appears new and not obvious. It is reasonably easy to decide whether a supposed invention is new—the examiner has only to read the claims of the specification and look in the earlier documents for anything falling within those claims. Deciding whether an invention is obvious, on the other hand, is always difficult and with nothing to go by except what appears in patent specifications becomes almost impossible. Naturally, then, examination for obviousness produces some odd objections: the only thing an examiner can do is turn the application down and see whether the applicant's patent agent can produce a convincing answer to the objection.

When examining for obviousness, the examiner considers only earlier specifications already published at the date when the application was filed (or the date of an earlier application giving priority, if there is one). But in considering whether the invention is actually new, he must look also at specifications published after but already on file at that date: in relation to novelty only, these are treated as if already published. This makes things complicated, see below.

DELAY IN APPLICATION

If a reasonable specification was filed with the application for a patent (either the application actually proceeded with, or an earlier one made here or abroad—see above, "Successive applications,") nothing after that counts in deciding on the validity of the patent. This is the main reason for getting an application in as soon as enough is known about the invention for a specification to be drawn up. If there is delay, some competitor, here or abroad, working along the same sort of lines may in the meantime publish some description, or market something, or make some patent application, that will make it difficult or impossible to get a valid patent at all. Or the inventors themselves may let out enough information to invalidate their own patent: by samples shown to the trade perhaps, or by some note in a trade journal. Too often inventors let the cat out of the bag too soon. Even a single non-confidential disclosure to one person anywhere in the world is enough to destroy a subsequent patent. And a single use from which it is possible without undue skill to work out the nature of the invention is also enough. There is a particularly acute problem in the case of inventions which need some sort of public trial. There is no special protection for such trials, so if you can work out the nature of the invention from such a trial there will be prior disclosure (*Lux* v. *Pike*, 1993). Public trial which does not enable a skilled man to know the secret of the invention is, in itself, all right (*Quantel*, 1991).

That problem can be dealt with (as has been explained) by getting on file an informal patent application that is good enough to support the claims in a proper application filed in due course. But getting priority in this way will not stop a competitor working along similar lines—and it is remarkable how often competitors are found to have been working along similar lines—from getting his own patent. If a competitor has a patent covering the same thing, it may be impossible to work the invention without a licence from him. To invalidate rival patents, it is necessary either to have made the invention public or to have filed a patent application (in this country, or an international or European one "designating" this country) which is in due course published. But it will seldom be safe to allow publication of an application intended only to give priority: it might anticipate the inventor's own later application too. So: not only should the first, informal application be filed as soon as practicable, the formal application should be filed as soon as practicable too.

EXAMINATION PROCEDURE

If an examiner sees an objection to the specification or the claims (or considers the whole thing unpatentable) he writes to the applicant's patent agent stating his objection. The applicant must show that he is wrong, or alter the specification or claims, or abandon the application. (If he and the agent cannot agree, the matter will go to a Principal Examiner, and if necessary the applicant can appeal from him to the Patents Court.) This is for a British application. The position is similar in the EPO.

GRANT AND REVOCATION AFTER GRANT

If and when all objections have been overcome, the applicant must pay another fee, and the patent will then be granted. Its owner may then start to sue for any infringements that have occurred since that application was published. The patent may still be revoked, however, either by the Patents Court or by the Patent Office, if anyone can show (in effect) that it should not have been granted. (Such an attack on the patent is almost certain to be made if the patentee sues for infringement, as part of the defence to the action.) The grounds for revocation differ markedly as between old and new patents: see the Note at the end of this chapter. To attack a patent in the Patent Office will be much cheaper than attacking it in the court, mostly because of the different way in which the evidence is provided; but an attack in the Patent Office will often be less likely to succeed.

EPO OPPOSITIONS

There is one feature of the EPO system which calls for special mention: the mis-named "opposition." Within nine months of grant, anyone can "oppose" the patent in the EPO, that is to say, seek its revocation. If successful, an opposition will knock out the patent everywhere. Unfortunately the opposition procedure (which has one tier of appeal, where, oddly, fresh arguments and evidence are common) is extraordinarily slow, leaving the fate of the patent or the scope of eventual claims uncertain for many years. (Of course this may operate to a patentee's advantage.) Moreover the procedure is, at least to those used to the Anglo-Saxon system, crude and uncertain. It proceeds almost exclusively on paper with oral hearings seldom lasting more than a morning. There is no real method of assessing evidence—assertion of technical fact by an advocate is common and accepted. "I discussed the case with an engineer yesterday and he said. ..." seems to do as well as a sworn statement. There is no cross-examination or discovery. Quite often parties are permitted to take the other by surprise at a hearing, for instance by producing an exhibit "out of the hat." The slowness of the opposition system can have serious effects on enforceability too. In many European countries the courts will not enforce the patent or hear revocation proceedings whilst there is an opposition pending, though there is the later advantage that considerable respect is given in those countries to a patent which has survived EPO opposition. Here our courts will not stay proceedings pending determination of an opposition, unless the final result of that opposition (on appeal) is imminent. Moreover a patent which has survived an EPO opposition is not treated differently from any other patent by our courts, which decide the case using their own judgement on the evidence. The possibility of an EPO opposition is a factor in favour of a national application. Some companies, particularly US companies, are now reconsidering previous policies of using the EPO as a preferred patenting route. The EPO has said that it will hurry things up in urgent cases (both before grant or in oppositions). However, to a patentee wanting his patent granted or to an opponent wanting his opposition determined, the Office's sense of urgency seems rather like that of the man who thinks that *manana* conveys too great a sense of haste.

COST AND PERIOD OF PROTECTION

A patent granted in London covers the whole United Kingdom, and proceedings upon it may be brought in the English, Scottish or Northern Irish courts as may be appropriate. The patent is kept in force by annual renewal fees, increased from time to time to keep pace with inflation, for a total period of 20 years from filing. The inventor has also to pay the fees for filing, search, examination and grant already mentioned. There will also be the modest charges made by the patent agent who drafts the specifications and negotiates with the Patent Office. Foreign patenting will add very greatly to the cost.

Money can of course be saved by not paying renewal fees and letting the patent lapse, but patents that are not kept up for their full term are seldom much use: since all a patent can do is to stop other people using the invention it will not be of value until the invention has reached the stage where other people want to use it. Few inventions are profitable quickly enough to tempt others to infringement in their first years; indeed, many inventions of importance seem seldom to be very profitable until quite late in the life of any patent covering them. Of course, it is often impossible to tell at the beginning what an invention is likely to be worth and, in doubtful cases, it will be better to take out a patent just in case; even so, the published figures suggest that many useless applications are filed.

GRANT AND OWNERSHIP

Inventors these days are usually employees of some company, and as a rule the company either is entitled to the patent under their service agreements or it buys them out before or soon after the application is filed. Arrangements can be made for the patent to be granted to whoever actually owns it—usually a company—even where the application is made by the actual inventor. Once a patent has been granted it can be bought and sold much like other property, provided the disposition is made in writing and the transaction is registered at the Patent Office. The name of the current owner can usually be found from the Register, because failure to register could lose him some of his rights. The names of the applicants appear on the printed copies of the specification sold by the Patent Office.

A sale or other disposition of the patent may be effective in law if made by those whose names appear on the register of proprietors, whether or not it "really" belongs wholly or in part to someone else. If, therefore, the inventor (for example), or the promoters of a company which is to exploit the invention, wish to retain some control over a patent, it may be wise for them to be registered as part proprietors.

PATENT AGENTS

In practice, the work of negotiating with a Patent Office (UK or EPO) is done by patent agents, whose profession it is. They also draw up nearly all specifications and are concerned in nearly all Patent Office proceedings and so on. It is theoretically possible for an inventor to do everything himself without professional help, but if a patent is worth applying for at all, the difference made by practised drafting of the specifications and skilled negotiation with the examiner will be worth far more than a patent agent's fees. Furthermore, current application procedure is so complex that it is best left to experienced professionals.

THE GROUNDS ON WHICH A PATENT MAY BE DECLARED INVALID

The grounds on which patents may be held invalid (by the courts or by the Patent Office) are different for new and for old patents. These grounds are of great practical importance. It should always be borne in mind that while it is often fairly easy to decide whether a patent is infringed or not, it is very seldom easy to decide whether a patent is valid. Thus whenever there is a question of enforcing a patent by court proceedings, the question of validity may be the most important one in the case. It will be seen that while some of the grounds set out below affect the patent as a whole (insufficiency of instructions, for instance) others affect only the claims as such. Where this is so, it is possible for some of the claims to be valid (or even, to be partly valid) although others are invalid. Such a position gives rise to difficult procedural problems, but for most purposes the important question then is: is any claim that has been (or will be) infringed a valid claim? The other claims matter much less.

Grounds affecting both new and old patents

These are the grounds:

1. Lack of novelty: That a claim of the specification includes something which had been published in this country (or used here, either publicly or secretly, but not purely by way of experiment) before the priority date of that claim. The claim is then said to be "anticipated" by the prior publication or prior user (the "prior art").

2. Obviousness: That claim includes something that was obvious, at its priority date, in view of what had already been published or publicly used in this country before.

This ground also is closely connected with width of claim, so tends to affect only the "main" claims of a patent.

3. Insufficiency: That the Specification does not give clear and full enough instructions to enable a skilled man to carry the invention into effect.

It is possible for there to be insufficient instructions to carry some claims into effect, but sufficient for others; but, generally speaking, a specification tends to be sufficient for all claims or insufficient for all.

4. Obtaining: That the patent was granted to someone not entitled to it.

This objection takes a rather different form with old patents (that the applicant for the patent was not qualified to apply, or that it was obtained in contravention of the rights of whoever alleges the invalidity); but the effect is much the same.

5. Not an invention: That the alleged invention is not the sort of thing that can be patented at all.

Grounds affecting "new" patents only:

Publication abroad: that the invention is not new, or is obvious, in the light of the things published or used outside this country.

Wrongful amendment: That the specification has been altered, so as to disclose something not disclosed in the specification when it was first filed, or has been altered since the patent was granted to make the claims cover something they did not cover before.

Grounds affecting "old" patents only:

1. Prior claiming: That the invention (so far as claimed in some claim of the Complete Specification) is already the subject of a valid claim of earlier priority date in another patent.

2. Ambiguity: That it is uncertain what a claim means.

3. Illegality: "That the primary or intended use or exercise of the invention is contrary to law." (A patent for an improved way of forging bank notes, for instance.)

4. Inutility: That the invention (or some forms of it) will not work.

5. Lack of basis for claims: That the claims are wider than is justified by what the specification discloses.

6. Non-disclosure of patentee's best method: of working the invention, that is.

7. False suggestion: That the patentee got his patent by making a false statement.

Note: Inventions by Employees

Not all inventions made by employees belong to their employer: it depends on circumstances. Unless the employee's service agreement makes some special arrangement, more favourable to him—an agreement less favourable to the employee is ineffective, except in relation to inventions made before 1978—what governs the matter is whether or not it was the employee's job to make that sort of invention. If so, it belongs to the employer (just as a workman may be employed to make boots, which then belong to the employer, not the workman). If not, it belongs to the employee (even though he may have made it in his employer's time and misappropriated his employer's materials for the purpose). There is no half-way house, except by special agreement; so that if the invention does not belong to the employer, the employee can demand a royalty for its use or even refuse permission to use it. Inventions made before the employment began, or after it stopped, do not belong to the employer.

In deciding what the employee's job was, his general position is naturally crucial. An engineering draughtsman, for instance, is normally expected to improve the design he is drawing out if he can (although a radically new idea may be outside the scope of his employment even though sparked-off by something connected with his work). A factory hand is not normally expected to invent at all. Directors may well be in a position where anything connected with the company's business belongs to the company: by and large, a director must never profit at his company's expense. (The English agent of a foreign engineering concern has been held to be in that sort of position, too).

Sometimes, there is a special agreement, under which an employee-inventor not merely applies for a patent jointly with his employer (which in itself means nothing) but actually owns his share of the patent. Inventors should note (a) that sort of agreement is best put into writing, and (b) that the owner of a half-share in a patent cannot (unless the agreement specially says so) do anything with it except himself work the patent—something his employer may be able to do but he will not. (Forming a company to do it is not working the patent: the company will need a licence from both patentees). Such agreements should be vetted by a solicitor—on both sides.

If the employer does particularly well out of a patented invention made by an employee, the employee can apply (to the Court, or to the Patent Office) to be awarded a fair share of any "outstanding benefit" the employer has got from the invention: unless the rewarding of employees for that sort of invention is already covered by a collective agreement. To qualify for an award, the invention must have been made (not merely patented) after mid-1978; and people who were employed mainly abroad when they made their inventions cannot apply. In practice this provision has had little effect. One of the problems is that the Act speaks of the *patent* rather than the invention being of "outstanding benefit". Thus if an employer merely saves himself some money by using the invention, he has not received any benefit from his patent.

Note: Sources of The Law

For new British patents and European patents covering the United Kingdom, the law is set out in the Patents Act 1977, and the Rules made under it; but this needs to be read in conjunction with the European Patent Convention of 1973 (see s. 130 (7) of the 1977 Act). The voluminous documentation embodying the new law is to be found in the loose-leaf *Encyclopedia of UK and European Patent Law*. The sections of the Act on international applications need to be read in conjunction with the Patent Co-operation Treaty of 1970 which set up the system. "Old" patents, apart from modification in the Schedules to the 1977 Act, are governed by the Patents Act 1949. The modifications are fairly extensive; but still the basic law is the old law. For this, see published textbooks: *Blanco White on Patents* (5th ed., 1983), the *Encyclopedia* or *Terrell on Patents* (13th ed., 1982).

Note: Security Restrictions

Applicants resident here must apply to patent here (and wait six weeks) before making a patent application abroad, unless our Patent Office permits otherwise. This applies to European and International applications too (they can all be made through our Patent Office), and to most "follow-up" applications as well as the original one for an invention.

Note: History of Patents

The English patent system, from its earliest foundations in the Middle Ages, has been based on the principle of rewarding education with monopoly. In the fourteenth and fifteenth centuries, grants of letters patent were made to encourage European skilled workers to come to England and teach the largely agricultural and trading English industrial methods. Often the grant of letters patent was conditional on the grantee providing practical training for a number of native apprentices in the working of the inventions. Until the early seventeenth century it was very difficult to challenge these monopolies in the courts since to do so was regarded as evidencing a lack of proper respect for the sovereign's authority. The royal prerogative to grant patents was widely abused as a source of crown patronage, and the Statute of Monopolies (1623) confined the legitimate exercise of the prerogative power to grant patents to the true and first inventor in respect of the sole working or making of "any manner of new manufactures ... which others at the tyme ... shall not use." It also set a limit to the time for which the monopoly could be granted at 14 years. That statute (much of which is still in force for pre-1978 patents forming the basis for modern patent law) says that the grant of letters patent shall be permitted provided also that "they be not contrary to the law nor mischievous to the state, by raising prices of [commodities] at home or hurt of trade, or generallie inconvenient."

It was not until the eighteenth century that the specification (*i.e.* the description of the invention) became important as providing the educational function of the patent and also in defining the scope of the monopoly claimed. Until then, the subject matter of the patent was usually described in very broad and general terms and the patentee was probably in a relatively strong position to beat off infringers (for whom the punishment could be imprisonment). During the eighteenth century it was established that the grant of the patent would be made conditional upon the patentee's filing a specification of his invention within six months of grant, which would show that the invention existed, telling the public how to work it, and showing what the claimed invention was. The system whereby a potential patentee had to file a specification upon application for a patent dates from 1852. The official search to determine whether the invention had already been published was introduced in 1905.

NOTE: FURTHER READING ON THE HISTORY OF THE PATENT SYSTEM

Hulme, *The History of the Patent System*, 12 Law Quarterly Review, 141 (1896). Hulme, *The History of the Patent System*, 16 Law Quarterly Review, 44 (1900). Fox, *Monopolies and Patents* (University of Toronto Press, 1947). Dickens, *A Poor Man's Tale of a Patent* (a sceptical nineteenth century view).

4

HOW MUCH USE ARE PATENTS?

THE IMPORTANCE OF VALIDITY

OF the patents that are challenged before the courts of law, some are found to be invalid. Since most lawsuits about patents cost at least tens of thousands of pounds and the larger part of the cost falls on the loser, this is a serious matter for owners of patents. (The owner of a patent can insure against the risk of having to sue infringers, and some do.) It does not, however, follow that patents are useless; rather this is a measure of success that patents have. It is expensive to challenge the validity of a patent even if the challenge succeeds, and it is hardly ever possible to be sure beforehand that the challenge will succeed. Indeed, at present, though the position may change, it is not common for patents to be held invalid. In the ordinary way, therefore, it is a better proposition commercially to make something outside the "claims" of the patent, than to risk an action for infringement of them. As a rule, it is only the most important patents that are attacked, and even then the attacker will try to find a design that escapes at least the more impressive claims as far as possible. The great majority of patents go through their lives in peace, with nobody really convinced they are valid, but nobody prepared to take the risk of infringing them. Commercially they are just as useful as if they had been valid. Thus, even an invalid patent is often valuable enough to make it worth while keeping on bluffing until the bitter end. And there is a lot of truth in the old adage "a weak patent in strong hands is worth more than a strong patent in weak hands."

EVADING PATENTS

(a) By "designing round"
A more serious problem is that of the competitor who avoids infringement of a patent. It is much easier to say why a particular patented device is successful and what else would be successful when a product using that device has been on the market for some time, than

it was when the specification of the patent was drawn up. The longer a patent lasts the greater the experience at the disposal of competitors. Yet the patent agent who makes out the specification must foresee what in ten or 20 years' time other manufacturers are likely to want to do, and must frame his "claims" so as to include all these future activities—while at the same time excluding anything that has been published before. In practice, what he does is to guess which features of the new product are going to be important to its success, and make his claims cover whatever combinations of those features are not found in the earlier specifications found by the examiner at the Patent Office. If he guesses right, the patent should be valid and fairly hard to "design round." If he guesses wrong, it will be found later on either that he has "claimed" something only trivially different from the subject of an earlier patent (in which case the new patent will be invalid for obviousness), or that he has confined the monopoly to things having some feature that is not essential—in which case competitors may be able to avoid infringing the patent by omitting that particular feature. Though the courts may disregard features shown not to be practically significant, this cannot be relied on to happen. Indeed mostly the courts say that the patentee must have regarded the feature as significant for otherwise he would not have put it into his claim. Patent agents would be able to guess right more often, if their clients supplied them with more and better information to base their guesses on. As it is, most patents are proof against casual imitators, but not all are proof against a determined attack by competent designers backed by proper legal advice.

(b) By making something "old"

A list of the earlier specifications considered important by the Patent Office examiner in any particular case can be obtained from the Office and one way of avoiding a patent is to go back to one of these earlier inventions. The owner of the later patent is then in a dilemma: if the rival product is within the "claims" of his specification, then his invention is not sufficiently different from the earlier one and his patent must be invalid. A defendant who says his product is old or an obvious development of what is old is said to be raising a "Gillette" defence, named after an old case, *Gillette* v. *Anglo-American*, 1913. There the defendant's razor closely resembled an old razor and the judges said there was "no patentable, no invention step" between the defendant's and the old razors. If the owner of the patent has made a real technical advance and his specification is skillfully drawn, his product should have a sufficient commercial advantage over earlier designs and his patent will protect that advantage. If, however, as so often happens, he is only the first to interest the public in an idea and not the first to make it technically successful, then competition based on earlier designs may be very damaging. *Hallen* v. *Brabantia*, 1989, is a good recent example of this sort of thing. The plaintiff had been the first to put the "non-stick" material PTFE ("Teflon") onto a type of corkscrew called a "self-puller": when you go on turning, the cork rises up out of the bottle. But self-pullers were old and a Frenchman had put PTFE onto another type of corkscrew to help get the screw into the cork. It was obvious thereafter that PTFE would improve the "getting-in" of any kind of corkscrew, including self-pullers. So even though the plaintiff was the first to make PTFE self-pullers commercially attractive, he had no valid monopoly in them. No system of patents can stop competition of this sort: the commercial innovator of this kind must rely upon the commercial advantages of being first, ideally a good trade mark, and helped perhaps by patents on minor features and design rights to make it impossible for rival products to look the same as his.

As ways of avoiding patents go, this method of digging up an old design is reasonably safe and has the advantage in theory that there is no need to do any patent search to see if what is being done is safe. But it is never completely safe. If what is now made is exactly what was made (or described) before the patent, then certainly any claim that covers it must be invalid. Nearly always, though, some alteration in the old design will be needed, if only to make it suitable for production. Then a quite different question arises, whether the changes to the old design were obvious changes to make before the date of the patent. The answer may easily be, that they became obvious changes to make only when the owner of the patent had shown that there was a market for something close to the old design. But if that is so, it is possible for the patent to be both valid and infringed.

Most firms will prefer not to take this risk unless the matter is of real commercial importance, so that in the ordinary way the patent will be almost as useful to its owner as if the earlier design had never been published. As we saw in Chapter 2, the value of a patent may depend greatly on its not being too important.

LICENSING

The general principle

So far we have only considered patent monopolies as a means of keeping imitations off the market. There is another way of exploiting a patent: the grant of licences. If the patent is valid, the manufacture, importation, sale or use of a patented article (or of articles made by a patented process or machine) are each only lawful if the patentee gives permission for them. Such permission is what is known as a "licence." Subject to the exceptions mentioned below, a patentee can charge what he likes for the licence and make what rules he likes for its exercise. For those who do not wish to manufacture under the patent themselves, and for many who do manufacture themselves, this is the normal way of making money out of a patent.

Permission to use and sell is implied where the patentee made the product himself or licensed its making, but even so the permission may be given subject to express limitations or conditions. Anyone who buys the article knowing of these conditions must either comply with them or risk being sued for infringement of the patent. Not every sort of limitation or condition, though, is allowed.

The main restriction here arises from the EC rules about "free circulation": once a patented article has been put on the market in the EC, by the owner of the patent or with his licence, he cannot stop its subsequent sale anywhere in the EC. This means, in particular, that although it may be allowable to restrict a licensee to manufacturing under the patent only in one EC country, the patent cannot be used to stop the things he makes being sold throughout the EC. Even a licence to manufacture in a single country only has to comply with some complex and not very comprehensible regulations in order to satisfy the EC.

Our own law also contains some specific restrictions on the terms there can be in licence agreements: in particular, the licensee cannot normally be compelled to buy unpatented materials from the licensor (though he may be given preferential terms if he does, so long as the EC rules mentioned above are not transgressed); and the licensee cannot be stopped from putting an end to the licence once the original patents have expired (though he can, sometimes, and subject again to EC rules, be required by the licence to stop manufacturing if he does).

5

IMPORTANT INVENTIONS

INTRODUCTION

EVERY now and then, somebody makes a really important invention. As a rule nobody knows this has happened until too late, and it is found either that the man who made the crucial step did not bother to apply for a patent at all, or that his application was considered just as a matter of routine, so that he got the sort of patent we discussed in the last chapter: a patent that would do very well to cover some minor improvement, but will stand neither a determined challenge to its validity nor a determined attempt to escape from its "claims." In that case, the invention can be used by any one prepared to spend a little time and money upon research and rather more upon litigation. Sometimes, though, the inventor—or the inventor's employer—knows he is on to a good thing. What should he do about it?

WHERE OTHERS HAVE TRIED

If the invention is one that a lot of people have been trying to make there may well be very little to be done about it, except get whatever patent the Patent Office will grant and hope for the sympathy of the court in due course. For in that case the files of the Patent Office will contain dozens or hundreds of specifications dealing with the subject, and some of them will almost certainly have come too close to the right answer for there to be much left to patent. In theory, of course, the failure of many other workers to make the invention is strong evidence that it was a good and patentable invention, rather than something obvious; but in practice, the drafting of valid claims that are broad enough to give real protection for the invention is impossible where there have been too many earlier proposals. Some big firms especially make a point of patenting every slight advance in research into such subjects; partly in the hope that if one of their competitors finds the answer they will have patents of their own important enough to bargain with, partly for the very purpose of

42

making it difficult or impossible for competitors to get valid patents. The independent inventor, hoping to make a large fortune by research in competition with the research departments of such large firms, is for this reason almost certainly wasting his time, however brilliant the work he is doing. He would probably make more money by research in some field that is specialised enough for his success not to be a serious challenge to his bigger rivals.

AN IMPORTANT INVENTION

Let us consider then the case of a manufacturer who is in possession of an invention that he believes is important, and that is unexpected enough to offer a chance of a really valuable patent. It will have to be a valid patent, for it is sure to come under hostile scrutiny as soon as its importance is understood; and it must have "claims" that are wide in scope, so that competitors cannot escape from it except by spending large sums upon research. It follows that attention will have to be paid to legal technicalities, which means extra trouble and extra expense in applying for the patent—though they will be trifling compared with the trouble of fighting a lawsuit later on, and the expense that will be incurred even if the suit is successful.

(a) The initial application

The first step will be the filing of an application accompanied by an informal specification. It will be worth giving more care than usual to the drafting of this, so as to be certain that it both includes as much detailed information as possible and foreshadows the claims that will be incorporated in the final specification. In this connection, it must not be forgotten that those claims will have to be broad ones: they must cover not only the actual machine or process that the inventor would like to see used commercially but also any alternative form of the invention that competitors may want to use—or that competitors may be prepared to use if compelled to do so by the need to avoid the patent. In order to be sure that such broad claims will hold as "priority date" the date of the original application, some basis for them must be laid in the original specification: both by indicating the general principles of operation of the invention, and by suggesting alternatives to whatever is actually described in detail in the specification. Many inventors dislike including descriptions of alternatives that they believe to be inferior, but it ought to be done. If the alternatives later turn out to be hopelessly inferior, they can be abandoned when the final specification is drawn up.

It may be desirable to file more than one preliminary application, so as to get the best priority for further discoveries made from time to time. As was explained in Chapter three, though, the definitive application should not be left too long, in case competitors try to patent something similar.

(b) Protection abroad

It will soon be necessary to consider patenting abroad: even a company not able to contemplate manufacturing abroad or bringing infringement actions abroad to protect an export market, may want to license foreign manufacturers and get something back that way. (Even a foreign manufacturer who is really interested mainly in "know-how" will often be unwilling to sign a satisfactory agreement, unless there are patents in his home country to hang the agreement on.)

First, Europe. The initial application can be filed here: a British application can found priority in Europe as well as a European one can. But before any application is filed that is meant to be proceeded with, a decision will have to be taken whether in Europe to seek separate national patents, or a European patent: or both. (See Chap. 3; and note that if both British and European patent applications are wanted, either a single international application must be made for them—see below—or both applications must be filed on the same day; otherwise one will anticipate the other.) In the case of a really important invention where patenting costs are only a minor factor the sensible thing to do is to go via both national and the EPO routes.

In countries outside the European system, the initial British application (or applications) can again be used to give priority. Almost all industrial countries are parties to an international convention (called the "Paris" Convention) concerning patent rights, which allows residents of any such country to file a patent application at home, and then within a specified period (normally 12 months) to file corresponding applications in the rest of such countries "as of" the date of his home application. Most countries place applications under the convention at some disadvantage. It might therefore seem desirable to make entirely separate applications at home and in certain foreign countries. But the European system of informal applications is exceptional, so such foreign applications would normally have to wait until a specification corresponding to our final specification could be prepared. This would involve a loss in priority. Further, some countries refuse altogether to patent otherwise than under the convention an invention that is already patented elsewhere. The normal practice is consequently to make foreign applications by means of the convention, accepting the disadvantages that result and ignoring the smaller countries which are not parties to it.

As we said in Chapter 3 it is possible to avoid the trouble and expense of preparing and filing separate applications for all countries where patents are wanted by filing an international application. So the inventor must chose whether to use this route for his application rather than separate national routes.

(c) The specification .

The final specification must be filed within 12 months of the first application, in any case, and unless foreign patenting is to be handled entirely by an international application will have to be ready long enough before then for specifications based on it to be filed at Patent Offices abroad within the 12-month period. Before the filing, the inventor should set to work to discover the secret of his own success and, when he has, should put the answer into a further specification.

It was explained in the previous chapter that for a patent to be fully effective, the distinguishing features of the "invention" (as listed in the claims of the specification) must all be features that play a real part in the success of the new device. The system of guessing which features matter is too risky when the patent will be important: so the specification must be drawn up by someone who knows what the vital points are.

(d) The Patent Office examination

The applicant will not at this stage yet know whether his patent is going to be a satisfactory one. He will not know this until his invention has been compared with those in earlier specifications, and it usually pays in practice to leave the job of searching for these earlier documents to the examiners at the Patent Offices concerned. Nor can the claims of the specification receive their final form until the examiner's comments have been received. If the specification has been well drawn up the examiner may not have any serious objection to make: he will almost certainly find something to comment upon in the wording of the specification. It does sometimes happen that his search produces nothing. This is inconvenient since it leaves the patent agent handling the case in the dark as to what earlier documents there are. To avoid this, the draftsman will sometimes "draw a search" by including initially a broader claim than he considers himself entitled to. Further, it may be advisable to make even the most half-hearted objection by an examiner an excuse for quite large alterations in the "claims"; for the claims are being framed less with a view to satisfying the examiner than with a view to what a judge may say later on. It may prove desirable in this country to frame the specification in a way to which the examiner will object; examiners are not trained lawyers, and have a lot of work to get through, and naturally tend to prefer standard patent jargon and standard forms of claim to anything new. This is fine for doubtful inventions, since the incomprehensibility of the jargon makes it harder for the patentee's competitors to decide whether the claims mean anything or not, are anticipated or not. A court, less conditioned to the jargon, may take a different view of it. Besides, sooner or later new sorts of claim become desirable: claims for important biotech inventions and such like. There has to be a first of such things, and any good examiner will probably notice and question it.

If necessary, disagreements with the examiner must be disposed of by obtaining a "hearing," that is, by going to the Patent Office and arguing the point out with one of the higher officials. If he in turn is not persuaded it will be necessary to appeal to the Patents Court or the EPO Board of Appeals depending on which patenting route has been taken.

(e) Amendment

The examiner's search usually uncovers a representative collection of the published documents on which later attacks on a patent might be based, while the applicants themselves will usually know what sort of thing was made and used in this country up to the date of the application. Sometimes, however, a publication will turn up later on which was not considered when the specification was drafted, and which seriously threatens the validity of the patent. Or it may turn out that something too close to the claims of the patent was publicly used, either in this country or abroad, before the date of the application, the applicants not knowing of it (or omitting to mention it to their patent agent). The validity of the patent can then only be secured by "amending" the specification: that is, by altering the claims so as to narrow them down until they no longer include whatever it is that has turned out to have been unpatentable. Amendment can be left until the last minute, when court proceedings about the patent have started or are contemplated, but it is nearly always far better to amend as soon as the patent is found to be invalid; amendment is easier then (for it is less likely to be opposed) and fewer problems will arise afterwards. In particular, the patentee ought not to leave in his specification claims he knows or suspects may be invalid, and if he does so, when in due course he does apply for amendment, he may be required to explain the reasons for delay. This occurred in *Wilkinson Sword* 1975 where the explanation was accepted, and *Smith Kline & French* v. *Evans*, 1989 where it was not. In the case of a patent whose specification was drafted without especially full investigation of the invention and its potentialities for future developments, the specification is likely to be defective anyway by reason of matters not known to the draftsman, so that amendment is worth considering as soon as the patent is found to be important enough to be worth spending money on.

Amendment of the specification requires the permission of the Patent Office or, if the patent is the subject of an action pending in the court at the time, of the court. Permission to amend is not very difficult to obtain provided the patentee moves quickly once he knows of the need to amend and has not originally had greedily wide claims. It is not possible to widen the "claims" (so that nothing can infringe after amendment unless it infringed before) and it is not possible to add completely new matter. (So it is not possible, for instance, to cure by amendment a failure to give adequate instructions to carry out the invention, nor to add a new feature which was not mentioned in the specification and has since been found essential to the working of the invention. One may properly cut a claim down, to exclude something old or obvious, but it is dangerous to try to include an explanation of the reasons for what has been done.) Further, amendment of the specification may make it impossible to recover damages for infringements that took place before amendment. The result is that while the power to amend is very useful it is a poor substitute for successful drafting of a specification in the first place.

The Action for Infringement

The first action in which a patent is involved is vital for that patent— such an action is usually fought once and for all. If the patentee loses, it means either that his patent is found invalid and the grant is revoked or that the claims of the specification are declared to be too narrow to cover the articles the defendant is making. In the former case there is no longer any patent, in the latter everyone in the industry now knows how to get round it. If he wins, on the other hand, his competitors will probably respect that patent in future: there are always other things to make and sell that do not involve a patent action. Furthermore, if the patent is held valid, the patentee will receive a "certificate of contested validity," which, while not forbidding others to challenge the validity of the patent or to claim they are not infringing it, will make it extra expensive for them if they lose. (The actual effect of a certificate is to entitle the patentee, if he wins another action on that patent, to ask for "solicitor and own client costs" instead of "standard costs" for the action. "Standard costs" are supposed to correspond to the reasonable amount it would be possible to spend in fighting the action (any doubts being resolved in favour of the paying party); "solicitor and own client costs" to what has actually been spent. The difference, for a patent action, may be very large.)

Delayed actions

It was emphasised in Chapter 1 that, in most cases, if a patent action is going to be fought at all, the sooner it is started the better. Equally, there are cases where an action should not be started at all. For example, a patent of dubious validity may be of considerable commercial value, being respected by most competitors. If someone does pluck up enough courage to infringe it, it may be better to buy him off, with a licence at low rates (or even free of royalty) rather than risk suing. It may be better thus to buy off a whole series of competitors—a sort of game of sardines. If, on the other hand, the patent is probably valid, and infringers are not of great importance compared with those who respect the patent or pay royalties, it may be worth while waiting until the patent has almost expired and then cleaning up by demanding damages from infringers—rather than upsetting things by suing earlier. (In any case, where an infringer is not sued right away, consideration should be given to notifying him of the existence of the patent, to stop him pleading innocence later.) Again: suppose a competitor finds a way round the patent, and tries to patent his alternative. The immediate reaction of most businessmen is to attack his patent. It is the wrong reaction. The right thing to do is to encourage him to have his patent, to stop other rats using the same hole.

From the point of view of an intending imitator of the patented article, there is a serious risk that he may be allowed to make his imitation for several years and may then be faced with a claim for a very large sum in damages. He can bring an action before he starts manufacturing, asking the court to declare that the article he proposes to manufacture will not infringe the patent concerned. He may also ask the court to revoke the patent on the ground that it is invalid. The proceedings in either case are nearly as expensive as ordinary actions for infringement, and may be rather easier for the patentee to win.

THREATS

A threat of proceedings for infringement of patent can be very worrying to the recipient. Naturally, a manufacturer who infringes, or the importer of an infringing article made abroad, should expect the patentee to say "If you do not stop I shall sue you." But threats to a man's customers are another matter: they are unlikely to want to get involved, and will usually quietly stop buying his goods rather than face an action. So it is provided that anyone aggrieved by threats of an infringement action can sue for damages and for an injunction preventing further threats, "unless the defendant ... proves that the acts in respect of which proceedings were threatened constitute or, if done, would constitute an infringement of a patent"—and the patent is not shown to be invalid. But there is this exception, that if the only threat is to sue for making or importing something (or for using a patented process) no action lies. (Taken literally, this exception does not cover a threat to sue the manufacturer or importer for selling the goods concerned; but the courts will say that Parliament cannot have meant to be as silly as that.)

Since it is very seldom possible to be certain of proving that any particular act is an infringement of a patent, or to be sure that any claim in a patent specification will not be found invalid, this provision is a dangerous trap for unwary owners of patents.

COMPULSORY LICENSING

The owner of a patent ought to make use of his invention if he can; certainly he ought not to use his patent for preventing all use of his invention. In the hope of preventing such misuse of patents, provisions of one sort or another have for many years been inserted in the Patents Acts; in particular there have been provisions by which anyone who wants to use an invention and can show that the patents covering it are being misused in certain ways can apply to the Patent Office for a compulsory licence, enabling him to use those patents upon payment of a proper royalty. The application cannot be made for three years after the patent has been granted. Compulsory licence provisions have never proved effective, and the present ones are hardly ever used.

Patents are not in practice used for suppressing new ideas: the difficulty with anything really new is to get anyone to take it up. Stories about patents for everlasting lightbulbs or the like being bought by existing manufacturers to protect their existing business are apocryphal. The few applications for compulsory licences that are made are not concerned with inventions that have been suppressed, but with inventions that have already proved profitable—where the patentee wants to keep the profit to himself.

There is a special rule for "old" patents (ones applied for before mid-1978) in the last four years of their lives: here anyone can get a compulsory licence, at least for manufacture in this country, whether the patent has been misused or not. This provision was mainly of importance for pharmaceutical patents, but its application to these and to agrochemical patents has been abolished and the provision is now of lesser importance.

Supplementary Protection Certificates

Most of the life of a patent for a medicine may be exhausted before the safety authorities give permission to market. So the patentee may have spent a small fortune yet have very little monopoly period to recover his costs and make a profit. To deal with this there is a new EC Regulation and scheme. Under this, a certificate can be obtained which extends protection for a patented medicine (the one actually sold, not everything covered by the patent) for up to five years from normal expiry of the patent. The amount of extension is the period between application for the patent and first permission to market anywhere in the EC less five years.

"Improvement" Patents

If a patent proves really profitable, its owner will want to go on profiting from the invention after his patent expires. There is a way in which a monopoly in an important invention may be kept alive after the patent has come to an end, and that is by patenting large numbers of minor improvements to the original invention. Provided the patented improvements represent genuine development over the period during which the original patent is in force, and provided they are patented with determination and persistence, by the time the original patent expires a would-be imitator should be faced with this situation: that the article described in the original specification is too inferior to contemporary designs to be commercially saleable, while he cannot equal the newer models without risking an action for infringement of so many of the improvement patents, that he would almost certainly lose in respect of some patent or other. Even if he were to win the action on enough of the patents to let him go on manufacturing without any fundamental change in his design, the cost of fighting and losing the action as a whole would still take much of the profit out of his venture. For this reason the existence of a mass of improvement patents is often a sufficient deterrent to would-be imitators. The original manufacturer's position need not deteriorate with further lapse of time: he should always be some years ahead in design so far as patentable improvements are concerned, while the longer he keeps the field to himself the greater the advantage he has in manufacturing experience. His monopoly will last until some competitor comes along with the skill needed to "design round" the more dangerous patents and the courage to fight a patent action if necessary; how long this will be will depend as usual on the importance of the market covered by the monopoly, as well as on the rate at which he continues to devise new patentable improvements. In the past, such monopolies have sometimes lasted a long time.

Where the owner of the original patent is himself the manufacturer, the patenting of improvements presents no particular difficulty. Where, however, the main patent is exploited by licensing someone else to manufacture in return for payment of a royalty on production, the patentee will find it difficult not to lose control as soon as the original patent expires. For the developments on which improvement patents can be based will be made by the manufacturer, who will also have the practical experience; the new patents will naturally belong to him and the monopoly given by them will belong to him, too. Sometimes the manufacturer can be persuaded to agree that the original patentee shall become the owner of the improvement patents, but such arrangements are mostly illegal under EC law.

It is in general very difficult for an inventor who is not actively engaged in an industry to keep any substantial control over it by means of patents. Cases do still occur from time to time of inventors making large fortunes by using their inventions to build up large manufacturing businesses, while other inventors do well enough by selling their patents to existing firms and at the same time getting important posts with those firms as consultants or designers. The inventor who makes any large sum simply by the sale or licensing of his patents seems to be very rare.

TAXATION AND PATENTS

Patents are subject to special rules as to tax. Royalties are not allowable as business expenses of the manufacturer who pays them (so that they have to be paid out of taxed profits, if he has any profits to tax); instead, whoever pays the royalty out of taxed income should deduct tax before paying and may then keep it. (If he had no profits (*i.e.* no taxed income) to pay the royalties out of he must deduct the tax and hand it over to the Revenue.) Furthermore, capital sums paid for patents and patent licences (but not sums paid for know-how) are treated as income of the seller spread over a six-year period; this being balanced by allowing the purchaser annual allowances on what he has paid. (This is not quite as hard on inventors as it seems; for a professional inventor must reckon the proceeds of sale of patents as income anyway. It is hard on purely amateur inventors, but they have too few votes to matter.) The position of foreign patentees needs watching here: they naturally tend to demand that a British licensee agree to pay royalties (and even more, capital sums) free of tax. There are, in fact, agreements in force with most foreign countries under which a foreigner can get payment in full (in the case of royalties, the payer is compensated for the tax he would otherwise have deducted and kept); but the foreign patentee has to make the request, and licence agreements ought to be specially framed accordingly.

NOTE: PATENTS FOR DRUGS AND SIMILAR CHEMICAL COMPOUNDS

(a) Problems

The effective patenting of newly invented drugs and the like presents special difficulties. The fundamental problem is this. If the drug concerned is an entirely new chemical, its discoverer will be entitled to patent it; but just because it is entirely new, he will be unable to tell what related substances will be so similar in their effects as to be just as good. If he attempts to guess what other substances will work, he may well guess hopelessly wrong; if he confines himself to those he really knows about, his competitors (who have been told by his success what sort of thing to look for) will be able to market some related substance not covered by him. The preparation and trial of any new drug is a long job, and even the biggest research laboratories can try out only a few likely compounds at a time. To a certain extent the difficulty can be overcome by the power of amendment, but this is seldom a completely satisfactory answer. The inventor's main safeguard is the cost of testing and marketing a related substance; but if the drug is profitable enough, that may be worth doing.

Even worse difficulties face the man who discovers how to prepare a substance that already exists in nature (a vitamin, for instance, or something like penicillin); for there are bound to be other ways of doing the job that he cannot cover. Further, the man who discovers a new and valuable property of an old substance must be very clever to get any sort of patent at all, even to cover the stuff as sold. What he does, for instance, is to claim "a pharmaceutical dosage form" containing the old compound. Similar dodges can be devised for other types of invention. He should be able to get a patent to cover a process of using the stuff (not, though, use in medicine); but collection of royalties or finding out about infringements may be very difficult. To deal with discoveries of new medical or veterinary uses of known compounds, the Act has a new sort of patent: a patent for the compound "for" the newly discovered use. The intention is that the owner of the patent will then be able to sue anyone who sells the stuff, knowing or intending it to be used for the new treatment.

It might be thought that such inventions were particularly valuable and need to be specially encouraged; but the law is more concerned with restricting such patents than with encouraging them. It has in particular only recently been decided that the discoverer of a second unexpected medical use for a compound can get any patent for that at all.

(b) "Selection" patents

There is a special sort of invention that turns up fairly often in the field of chemistry, and leads to what are called "selection patents." When a new and valuable chemical compound is discovered—a new drug, perhaps, or a new sort of dyestuff—it will usually at once be apparent to a skilled chemist that innumerable other, closely related compounds may be as good or better. But there is usually still room for invention in making those compounds, one by one, and finding out which really are as good or better; and even more room for invention in seeing without making them all which others will be as good or better. This picking-out of the useful ones, from a large class which is already known in general terms, is known as "selection." The courts have laid down certain rules governing patents for such inventions: in particular, the specification must explain in what way the selected ones are better than the rest: and they must really be better, and better than almost all of the others. And, of course, this must be something that only an inventor could have foreseen. The rules were devised for old patents. They probably still apply though the EPO may have relaxed them somewhat.

NOTE: THE DEFINITION OF INFRINGEMENT

Most of the activities that amount to infringement are what one might expect: making, selling, importing, using a patented article; working a patented process or selling, importing or using the product. But it is also an infringement to "keep" the article or product; or knowingly to supply the means for working an invention, unless what is supplied is a "staple commercial product"— and even then it is infringement if the supply is intended to induce the recipient to infringe.

On the other hand, there are general exceptions: for things done privately and not commercially (it is not at all clear what "privately" means here: probably, "privately as distinct from commercially"); for experiments with the invention; for the making-up of individual medical prescriptions; for use by foreign ships and aircraft. There is also a special provision protecting those who used or prepared to use the invention before the priority date of the patent: they may go on doing what they did or prepared to do before. (This last provision is necessary, because use of an invention only invalidates a subsequent patent for it if the use makes the invention public, and manufacturing processes may well not be made public.)

6

CROWN RIGHTS AND SECURITY

The Crown's Right to Work Patents.

ANY government department may use, or authorise others to use, any patented invention "for the services of the Crown." Mostly, this means for the armed forces—although some drugs for British hospitals have been procured under these powers. The proprietor of the patent is entitled to compensation for any use by the Government in this way but he cannot prevent that use. If the invention was one that any government department knew about (otherwise than because its owner told them about it) before the patent was applied for, this does not of itself make the patent invalid but it disentitles the owner to compensation for any Government use.

Surplus patented articles, originally made for Government use, may be freely sold. So may articles confiscated by the Customs or Excise. So may medical supplies. During a war period and for war purposes, or for national purposes during a period of emergency, or in respect of inventions concerned with atomic energy, government departments may authorise anyone to sell such articles whether originally made for Government use or not—subject to the usual rights to compensation. The Government may also have weapons and munitions made here for allies, or the United Nations, and sell them to the government or organisation concerned. Except in these cases the Government has no right to authorise the sale of such articles without permission from the proprietor of the patent concerned.

If a firm authorised by the Government to use an invention is already licensed to do so by the proprietor of it, the royalties fixed by the licence need not be paid so far as the Government use is concerned. Such a licensee may still be liable to make some payments to the proprietor: guaranteed minimum royalties, for instance (see *No-Nail Cases* v. *No-Nail Boxes*, 1944). In general, however, the proprietor must rely on his right to demand compensation from the Crown. The amount of compensation, if it cannot be agreed, will normally be settled by referring the whole matter to the High Court. The crown is supposed to let inventors know that it is using their patents, but it tends not to (especially but not only where military secrets are involved). One of the inventor's main problem tends to be to find out what use if any is being made of his invention. The problem is at least in part caused by the fact that it is the Crown which is first supposed to decide whether it is using an invention. It will not "own up" even where it knows of the patent if it decides the scope of the patent does not cover what is being done or the patent is invalid. Naturally the patentee might take a different view but he does not get the chance.

There are similar provisions allowing Crown use of registered designs and design rights, though in practice this will not matter much.

KEEPING INVENTIONS SECRET

It is necessary to prevent the automatic publication of specifications of inventions of military importance. It is therefore provided, first, that such inventions may be communicated to and tried out by any Service department without prejudicing a subsequent patent application; and, secondly, that, if an application is made to patent such an invention, and if and so long as the appropriate Service department considers that it ought to be kept secret, the application for a patent will not be published, and though it will be examined it will not proceed to grant of a patent. Similar provisions apply to designs, and similar provisions apply to all inventions involving atomic energy, whether of military character or not.

Military inventions that the armed forces think good enough to use are just the ones they will want to keep secret. So the provisions giving inventors the right to be compensated for Crown use apply in such cases as if the patent were granted in the ordinary way. In addition, the Crown can if it likes compensate the inventor for the damage the secrecy does to him.

It would of course be useless to keep such inventions secret here if they were published abroad. For this reason, it is provided that no foreign patent may be applied for upon an invention made here, unless an application has first been filed here and six weeks have then elapsed without any direction being made that the invention should be kept secret.

7

INDUSTRIAL DESIGNS

INTRODUCTION

For many years our law has included protection for industrial "designs." Originally the general idea was to protect the artistic element in mass produced articles (shape or applied decoration or the like). The main mechanism for protection was supposed to be by a system of designs registered at the Patent Office—like a patent for an invention. But over the years both Parliament and the courts managed to produce a convoluted system as a result of the interaction between the law of registered designs and that of ordinary copyright. The problem arose because ordinary copyright in drawings could be infringed by indirectly copying an article made from them. This is easy enough to understand where a truly artistic drawing is concerned (*e.g.* of "Popeye," *King Features Syndicate* v. *Kleeman,* 1942) but seems odd in the case of purely mechanical items, such as an exhaust pipe. The whole business got out of hand: not only was the law complicated, it was unsafe to make things which were copies of, or based upon, very old articles. For instance Lego were using (successfully until final appeal) copyright to maintain a monopoly in their system even though the basic brick was designed in the 1940s. Absurd arguments as to eye appeal or otherwise of a Lego brick were deployed in all seriousness (*Interlego* v. *Tyco,* 1989). In the case of spare parts (exhaust pipes) it took the House of Lords to say, never mind ordinary copyright, you are allowed to make them (*Leyland* v. *Armstrong,* 1984).

So in 1988 Parliament tried to sort things out: whether it has succeeded remains to be seen; things are still pretty complicated. Under the present law there may be protection for industrial designs by registration and under also a new kind of right called a design right, created automatically and without any need for registration. The old protection via ordinary copyright has essentially gone for functional items, though of course it remains wrong just to photocopy design drawings. There are differences for designs made before the new law came in, in August 1989.

REGISTERED DESIGNS

These can be registered at the Patent Office if they are "new or original." This means not too like any previous design, registered or unregistered and does not mean simply that the design was all the author's own work (*cf.* the meaning of "original" in copyright law). Registration gives a true monopoly so, unlike copyright or unregistered design right, a defendant will infringe if he makes or deals in an article whose design is the same or not substantially different from that registered. But, as always, it helps if the defendant copied. The importance of registration has increased not only because other forms of protection have been lessened by the 1988 Act but also because you now can get up to a 25-year monopoly in your design (upon paying renewal fees every five years).

Apart from the requirement of novelty there are other limitations on what can be registered. Thus if aesthetic considerations are not taken into account by users (*e.g.* internal parts of a washing machine) or if the design is really for a principle or is purely functional (that is what the row in *Lego* was about) or if it is dependant upon the appearance of another article of which it forms a part (*e.g.* a car body panel) then it is not the sort of thing which can be registered.

Registering a design involves much less effort (and cost) than obtaining a patent. Normally some good photographs (from all angles) of a prototype three dimensional design are all that is needed. Two dimensional designs (*e.g.* a wallpaper or textile) would only need a sample. The biggest defect of the system is that it takes a while (about six months) for the registration to come through and in the case of some fields, such as some toys, the craze may be over before protection is obtained. This sort of design will however be protected by the unregistered design right. Another problem is that the protection must be sought (and the initial fees paid) before the design is made public, otherwise it will not be novel. This means that there are costs incurred before it is known whether the design has any value in the market. Typical fees for a design application (including a patent agent's fees) are £300–400. It is possible in simple cases to make the application without a patent agent, but, unless the applicant makes regular applications and knows what to do, it is best to use one.

Another advantage of the design registration system is that it can be used to claim priority in other countries (the applications abroad have to be made within six months rather than a year as in the case of patents). The international protection of designs will probably grow with the increasing trans-border nature of goods and markets. At present most other countries have design registration schemes, though the variation from country to country is quite marked, more so than in the case of patents. The EC has a proposal for harmonising design laws; this seems some way off.

DESIGN RIGHT

This is a wholly new kind of right for designs made after the 1988 Act came into force, so we have hardly any experience of what the courts will make of it. Its basis is the thought that even if a designer has not registered a design it is unfair if his design is copied. This went too far under the previous law but it was thought the designer ought to get something. The unregistered design right "DR" is the result. It only gives protection against copying.

A designer is given a DR in "any aspect of shape or configuration" (internal or external) of the whole or any part of an article. The design must be original (in the copyright sense of being the designer's own work, not copied) and must have been recorded in a design document or a physical article. There are special modifications (both as to the extent of the right and the nationality of origin) in relation to design rights in relation to the topography of semi conductor products, following our implementation of an EC directive on the subject. There are exceptions to DR: there is none in a method or principle of construction, or in a design which must fit some other article (*e.g.* a spare part) or must match some other article so as to form an integral whole (*e.g.* a body panel), or in a surface decoration. There is also an exception if the design is "commonplace."

At first sight therefore the DR is extremely powerful and pervasive. Almost any piece of design work will give rise to a DR. But the DR only lasts, at best, for 15 years from the end of the year when the design was first made. Earlier expiry occurs when the first marketing of the design takes place in the first five years of the life of the DR. Then expiry is at the end of the tenth year in which first marketing occurred. So in practice all a designer can get is ten years from first marketing; he is unlikely to be copied before then in any event, and his protection is cut down even more because, after five years from first marketing by the designer, his rivals can obtain a compulsory licence. So there may be quite a few cases where, when the copying starts a few years after first marketing, it will be doubtful whether a case could be brought to trial before the end of the five-year period during which an injunction can be had. In such cases the crucial question will often be: can the designer obtain an interlocutory injunction meanwhile?

There are obvious problems with the DR: for instance what does "commonplace" mean? Will it cover an article widely sold by just one manufacturer or must it be widely used in the trade? Where does a design have to be commonplace? Another difficulty relates to how close must a copy be to infringe? In the past the courts have made rather a mess of this (see the copyright drawings and photographs of the infringements in *LB Plastics* v. *Swish*, 1980). And in many cases there is a real difficulty; those where the defendant's design is really his own, influenced by the plaintiff's and the court has to decide where mere influence ends and copying begins. Moreover the courts have persistently failed to listen to a defendant who admits some degree of copying but says that what he copied was not the original part of a copyright work (see, *e.g. Merlet* v. *Mothercare*, 1982 and the *Lego* case). If the same attitude applies to DRs a designer may in practice be able to achieve lengthened protection. He will say (and probably be able to prove) that the defendant copied the latest version of his article. Even if the defendant has not got the original features of that, he may infringe its DR.

In practice, therefore, DR will be valuable to protect against slavish imitations early in the life of a product. It will help in fast changing fashion trades and will also give initial protection to a designer who has applied for registration of his design but is still waiting for it. DR cannot be used as a basis for claiming priority for foreign applications. Indeed unless a foreign country (outside the EC) recognises a similar right, their nationals are not entitled to DRs here.

It will obviously be important to keep drawings and prototypes for future enforcement. A well advised design based company would have a standard procedure for this, and for ensuring that the employment records of the design employees (or assignments from outside designers) are kept.

ORDINARY COPYRIGHT

For copyright works made after the 1988 Act came into force in August 1989 the scope for protection of industrial designs for most artifacts is limited. It is not an infringement to make a three-dimensional article directly or indirectly from copyright design drawings or models for a non-artistic work. However, in relation to works for surface decoration, all two-dimensional designs, such as fabric designs, and works which are designs for artistic works (*e.g.* drawings for a sculpture or a sculpture itself) the works may be copied in three dimensions after 25 years from the first industrialisation of the work. Prior to then it will be an infringement to copy. So, if the copyright drawing is for making an exhaust pipe then you can copy at once (subject, of courses, to design right). But if the drawing is for a textile design or for a sculpture or is of a cartoon character then you must wait 25 years.

PRE-AUGUST 1989 DESIGNS

The old regime of ordinary copyright applies to these for ten years, though with provision for a compulsory licence after five. So in the case of design drawings done before August 1989 it is an infringement to copy these, whether the product is functional or not. Licences will be available from August 1994 onwards. There cannot, of course, be any design right for these designs and registered designs only last for 15 years. The definition of the kind of design which could be registered is different too (*e.g.* no must fit or match exception), though this will only matter in marginal cases.

USE OF OTHER RIGHTS TO PROTECT DESIGNS

Some designs can be protected in other ways: for instance a design may in some cases also be a trade mark (*e.g.* the back of a playing card, *US Playing Card's Appn.*, 1907) or the scheme of colouration of medicinal capsules, *Smith Kline & French*, 1976. However the courts are careful to prevent these other forms of protection (which may be perpetual) from straying too far into the field of designs proper, so, for example, the shape of a bottle was held not to be registrable as a trade mark, *Coca-Cola*, 1986. Similarly plaintiffs sometimes try to use a passing-off action to protect a design, but generally fail. An example of this is *British American Glass* v. *Winton*, 1962 where the plaintiff tried to protect the design of his glass animals from copying but failed because he could not show that the customers cared which make of glass animal they were buying.

PART III

TRADE AND SERVICE MARKS AND UNFAIR COMPETITION

8

DIFFERENT DEGREES OF PROTECTION

PASSING-OFF

MOST European countries have some sort of general rule of law forbidding unfair competition. We have not: but most of the activities that such a rule would discourage run contrary to specific rules of English law. In particular we have a rule—and this is the subject of this Part of this book—forbidding the running of a business in such a way as to filch a competitor's trade by misleading conduct. The limits of this rule will be discussed in later stages; all that need be said here is that it is in essence a rule to protect business goodwill. It is difficult to define goodwill. Broadly it is that characteristic of a business which renders it permanent, which distinguishes an established business from one newly formed. In order to protect business goodwill, the law forbids any trader so to conduct his trade as to mislead customers into mistaking his goods for someone else's. Nor may he mislead customers into confusing his business as a whole with someone else's. It makes no difference whether it is other traders or the general public that are deceived; nor whether the deception is fraudulent or merely mistaken or accidental; not how it is brought about. This sort of deception is known as "passing-off"; anyone who suffers financial loss as a result of it is entitled to bring an action in the courts, claiming compensation for his loss, and asking for an injunction against continuance of the deception. Passing-off does not extend to non-deceptive encroachments upon goodwill: it is not passing-off to say honestly "my cola is as good as Coca-Cola but half the price." Passing-off is a powerful and effective remedy, provided only that the plaintiff is able to prove his case.

Where the case is clear on its face, or there is any serious indication that the defendant is dishonest, no difficulty arises, so long as the plaintiff moves quickly enough. He can ask for, and will be given a temporary injunction, putting a stop to the deception until the case can be tried—and that, almost always, is the end of the matter. The matter is settled and there is no need ever to have a full-scale trial. In cases that are less clear the difficulty of proof may be a serious one. So full trials of passing-off cases are rare. It is seldom possible to find anyone who has actually been deceived and will come and swear to it in court. (*Chelsea Man* v. *Chelsea Girl*, 1987, was one of those rare instances, the customers of the plaintiff coming to court out of loyalty.) The case must therefore be proved by showing that the circumstances are such that people are certain to be deceived sooner or later. This is not an easy task and much ingenuity by way of opinion polls and the like is expended on it, generally without success. The most important reason for registering trade marks is to make it unnecessary.

PASSING-OFF AND REGISTRATION OF TRADE AND SERVICE MARKS

Where there has been full registration of all trade marks, the sort of "passing-off" that involves imitation of trade marks or brand names can seldom occur without infringement of the trade mark registrations taking place too. Full registration of trade marks is not always easy or even possible; there are many legal pitfalls to be avoided. (Some of these are discussed in Chap. 11.) Where it is possible it enables the expensive and uncertain action for passing-off to be almost completely replaced by the cheaper and more reliable action for infringement of trade mark.

Passing-off and goodwill

In an action for passing-off the plaintiff must in practice prove that he has extensive enough goodwill for his goods to be recognised by members of the public; otherwise it will hardly be possible for people to be deceived when they come across similar goods put out by the defendants. It follows that the law of passing-off will protect established lines of goods of established businesses from imitation, but will not provide a shield behind which a new goodwill can be built up. Registration of a trade mark, on the other hand, is possible before the goods the mark is intended for are put on to the market at all. Since registration gives almost an absolute right to stop others from using that mark or a mark like it, goodwill can be built up behind the protection given by the Trade Marks Act. Similarly with service marks.

Why people sue for passing-off

Why, if suing for infringement is so much easier, does anyone sue for passing-off? (Passing-off actions are the more numerous, in fact.) There are several reasons.

Many businesses do not keep their trade marks fully and validly registered, so that resort to a passing-off action may always be necessary to cover flaws in the trade mark position. Further, passing-off can occur in cases that have nothing at all to do with trade marks: by the use of a name for a new company that is misleadingly similar to that of an old one; by the marketing of goods whose get-up is the same (in everything but the wording on the package) as that of an old-established line; and so on. And some activities are not regarded by the courts as "services" and fit ill with the notion of a trade in goods under the mark. For instance supermarket names are not registrable as service marks (*Dee*, 1990) and (save in the case of "own brand" labels) the name is not really used as a trade mark for goods: people do not think of "Sainsbury's" as being used for Heinz baked beans even though they sell them. Yet any trader who used "Sainsbury's" for a supermarket name would surely be stopped by passing-off. Other cases of passing-off which would not be covered by any form of registered mark are discussed in Chapter 13.

<h2 style="text-align:center">"PART A" AND "PART B" MARKS</h2>

There are two sorts of registered mark, those registered in Part A and those in Part B. Part A marks give the strongest rights, Part B gives lesser rights and the law of passing-off still less. The plaintiff who sues on a Part B mark is not required to prove that his goods or services are known to the public, and to that extent he is in the position of any registered mark owner; on the other hand, his action will fail, as a passing-off action will fail but an action for infringement of a Part A mark will not, if the defendant can show that although he used the plaintiff's mark it was not used in a way that was likely to mislead the public. "Part B" registrations are for this reason less valuable than the ordinary "Part A" ones, but they are easier to get and not uncommon for that reason. A mark registered in Part B may, when substantial goodwill has been attached to it, later be registered also in Part A, although often people do not bother to do this; the conditions for such re-registration in Part A are further discussed in Chapter 10.

Infringement of "A" marks

The rights given by "Part A" registrations are much wider than mere protection of a mark from imitation in the ordinary sense (how much wider, nobody quite knows). It now seems settled that you cannot use another man's "Part A" mark to advertise your goods even in a comparative way. Thus it is probably an infringement to say in an advertisement "my camera is as good as a Kodak but half the price," whether this is true or not. The law of passing-off gives no rights of this sort. So if you merely say such things (*e.g.* in a shop, or in the form of a "voice over" on a television advertisement) and they are true, the owner of the mark cannot complain. You do not infringe because you have not used the mark visually and there is no passing-off. The position may be different if what is said is untrue—see Chapters 14 and 15. There is a similar (and almost equally obscure) provision for service marks.

LITIGATION CAUSED BY UNCERTAINTY

Where a registered mark has been infringed, this is usually clear. Furthermore, a direct search of the trade marks register will show what marks are there, and so indicate whether a new mark can safely be used or not. Most instances of trade mark infringement happen through pure inadvertence, and are stopped as soon as the proprietor of the mark complains. But just because passing-off may occur in cases where there is nothing on any register, and in cases where there is room for a real difference of opinion as to the legitimacy of what is being done, when litigation does occur it is more likely to be a passing-off action than an action for infringement. The failure to register a mark may only too easily have to be repaired by the courts. It is worth noting, though, that quite a lot of litigation arises from something for which the law gives no remedy: the spoiling of marks by getting too close to them—that is, the case where a trader picks a mark that, although not close enough to a competitor's actually to be mistaken for it, is yet close enough for the public (who have no real interest in these things, anyway) not to bother to prefer one brand to the other. This, in effect, is one way of saying to the public: "Mine is just as good."

PROTECTION UNDER THE CRIMINAL LAW

Business activities involving obvious fraud are sometimes more easily prevented by criminal prosecution under the Trade Descriptions Act, and similar enactments, than by an expensive and troublesome civil action; for instance, in cases where goods are adulterated before sale. Prosecution is, however, unwise unless the case is very clear—

clearer than would be necessary for an ordinary action for an injunction and damages. See for example the "Spanish Champagne" case, where a civil action to stop sales of Spanish wine as "Spanish Champagne" succeeded (*Bollinger* v. *Costa Brava Wine Co.*, 1961) although a prosecution for it had already failed. This part of the criminal law is discussed in Chapter 15.

9

WHAT REGISTERED MARKS ARE FOR

INTRODUCTION

THIS chapter discusses, in more detail than the last, the rights of the registered proprietor of a mark. It refers primarily to marks "registered in Part A of the register"; the rules for "Part B" marks differ in certain ways which are discussed at the end of the chapter.

It is possible to resist any action for infringement of the rights given by registration mark by contending that the registration is invalid and asking for its cancellation. The rules deciding when a registration is valid and when it is not are discussed in Chapter 11. In the present chapter it will be assumed that all registrations are valid; in practice, most are.

GOODS OR SERVICES FOR WHICH THE MARK IS REGISTERED

The registration of any person as proprietor of a trade mark in respect of any goods gives him the exclusive right to use that mark in relation to those goods. It gives him no right to stop the use of the mark on goods for which it is not registered. In the same way, registration of a service mark protects only business in those services specified in the registration. In practice, a mark ought to be registered for any goods and services its owner uses it on or intends to use it for and also for all other goods or services of the same sort—that is, for what the law calls "goods (or services) of the same description," meaning roughly all that would be recognised by business people as belonging to the same trade. For detailed discussion of the words "of the same description," which occur in several parts of the Trade Marks Act, see especially *"Daiquiri Rum,"* 1969. Equally, a service mark should be registered for related goods—what the 1984 Act calls "associated" goods—and a trade mark should be registered for "associated" services.

Thus a trade mark used on three-hole razor-blades ought to be registered for all razor-blades and for razors as well. Most registrations are wider than this, but some firms make a practice of getting registrations that are far too narrow; for instance, "three-hole razor blades imported from Venezuela." This may or may not cover all goods on which the mark is likely to be used by its owner, so that he can put "registered trade mark" on his packet, and it will serve to stop other firms from actually registering marks for razor-blades that are too much like his; but it will be useless for preventing other firms from using his mark even on three-hole razor-blades, for it is most unlikely that they will import their goods from Venezuela. It will not even cover his own goods if he changes to a different source of supply or a different design of blade—as sooner or later he probably will. Just as bad would be registration for "a preparation of cream soap for use in shaving"; this would cover a shaving-cream made by the owner of the mark but would cover nothing else, possibly not even a different "preparation of soap for use in shaving" on which the mark was used by a competitor. Better a registration that is too wide; although it will be less effective or ineffective so far as the extra goods and services are concerned (this point is discussed later), it will, at least, protect the actual things its owner uses it for. Too many traders, after carefully getting registration for a new trade mark they mean to use on some new product, then change their minds, and alter the mark, or use it for a different product or some related service, without a thought as to whether their registration will still cover what they are going to do. It ought to be borne in mind that a business may want to expand and diversify, and will want to find its established marks available and protected over any new field of activity.

INFRINGEMENT

(a) By similar marks

A trade mark will be infringed by the use for the wrong man's goods or services not only of that mark itself, but of any other mark so nearly resembling it as to be likely to be misleading. The public cannot be expected to remember every detail of the trade marks on the various articles they buy and use; if two marks are so alike that members of the public having a general recollection of the one and seeing the other are likely to confuse the two, the second mark will infringe a registration of the first. A long list of pairs of marks which the courts have found to be too close or not too close will be found in

Kerly. As examples: "Vedonis Thermawarm" infringed "Thermawear" (customers sometimes wrote "Vedonis Thermawear," *Thermawear* v. *Vedonis*, 1982). On the other hand "Titch" (for small
staplers) was not too close to "Bostitch" (*Textron* v. *Stevens*, 1977).
In the latter case the two marks had been used for some time and there
was no confusion. Of course "titch" has a meaning (in this country—
Americans do not use it which may explain why the American plaintiff brought the case). If there had been no meaning the case would
probably have gone the other way. The decision rests, in the end, on
what the court feels when it looks at the two marks; and in difficult
cases, there is always a tendency to favour an established trade against
a new entrant who as yet has built up no real goodwill—but to hesit-
ate to interfere with a trade that has been going on for a considerable
time without complaint. In borderline cases, the decision will depend
on all those circumstances of the case that affect the likelihood of confusion; what sort of people the goods are sold to, for instance, and
whether they are likely to be ordered over the telephone. It depends
too on what particular features of the marks concerned stick in
people's memory, so as to be the features that matter in determining
whether two marks will be distinguished or confused: the "essential
features" of the mark, as they are called. So also the court will consider what is the basic idea of the mark. Thus "Watermatic" was held
to infringe "Aquamatic" (for toy pistols), the idea being the same although the sound is different; but "Kidax" (for clothing) was held not
too close to "Daks," the court not accepting that "Kidax" would be
confused with " 'kids' 'Daks.' " Now all this sort of thing depends
on what evidence the court has as to conditions in the trade and the
way the businesses concerned are carried on, something hard to fore-
cast before the case is heard. In general, though, it is necessary only to
look at the two marks to see whether there is an infringement, or no
infringement, or perhaps a borderline case. As we said before, this
certainty means that litigation is seldom needed to settle disputes.
One rule is that legitimate use of one validly registered mark will
never infringe another, so that a business which makes a practice of
applying to register all marks for the right goods or services before
using them is unlikely to run into difficulties over infringements of
other people's marks.

Unless there is a note on the register limiting a mark to particular
colours, it will not be affected by a change in colour. (On this point
our law is different from that of some countries.) If a word is registered in block capitals, the registration will be infringed by a use of
that word in lettering of any sort; the converse is, however, not

necessarily true. It is not possible to avoid infringement by adding other matter to a mark, so that if company A have registered a mark and company B use it on their own goods, they will infringe A's rights, however different the get-up of their goods from A's, and however prominently their own name appears on the packets or labels. This absolute character of the rights given by trade and service mark registration is essentially different from the rights to prevent misleading imitations by an action for "passing-off."

(b) Acts constituting infringement

It was indicated in the last chapter that the rights of the registered owner of a trade mark go far beyond simply preventing others from using his mark as a trade mark on their goods. Just how far beyond is not clear. The leading case on this point, *Bismag* v. *Amblins*, 1940; was about a catalogue published by the defendants, who were a firm of chemists. After explaining that their own products were at least as good as the nationally advertised brands, only cheaper, they set out in parallel columns a list on the left of widely advertised proprietary medicines with an analysis and the price of each, and a list on the right of their own corresponding products with identical analyses and much lower prices. The lay-out was such as to emphasise the correspondence between similar items in the two columns, and many of the proprietary brands in the left-hand column were referred to by registered trade marks. The Court of Appeal held that these registered marks were used "in relation" to the defendant's goods listed in the right-hand column as well as to the corresponding items on the left; the trade marks were consequently infringed. It is never safe for a trader to use any word or design, resembling anyone else's trade mark, either on goods which do not already lawfully carry that mark or in an advertisement relating to goods that do not lawfully carry that mark; and if the Court of Appeal interpreted the law correctly (the House of Lords doubted this in *Aristoc* v. *Rysta*, 1945) it is not safe to use such a mark in any context, unless it refers exclusively to goods lawfully carrying the mark. There is a very similar provision for service marks.

There are two schools of thought about the *Bismag* case: some say it is unfair for a trader to be able to advertise his unknown goods by latching on to a brand established and maintained at great expense by someone else. Others say that this is a competitive age. So, provided the first trader tells no lies, why should he not compare his goods with others, why should he not use fair "knocking copy"? Different

judges seem to belong to different schools. Some have devised spe-
cious distinctions from the *Bismag* case, particularly that there is a
difference between use of a trade mark and use of a company name
which happens to include that trade mark. For instance, in one recent
case Dell were allowed to compare their computers with those of
"Compaq Computers Limited" but not allowed otherwise to use the
word "Compaq" in their advertisements (*Compaq* v. *Dell*, 1992). In
another, Ever Ready were allowed to compare their batteries with
"the batteries sold by Duracell Limited" (*Duracell* v. *Ever Ready*,
1989). A layman would say that this sort of distinction is nonsense:
either you can compare honestly or you cannot. On the other hand,
there are recent instances of the application of the *Bismag* rule, for instance the Daily Mirror could not put an advertisement saying (in the
time of Mrs. Thatcher) under the *Sun* masthead "Yes, Prime Minister" and under the *Mirror* masthead "No, Prime Minister" ("*Sun*"
being a Part A mark) (*News Group* v. *Mirror*, 1989). And a perfume
company was not allowed even to give to its own sales agents a list of
the fragrances of its perfumes with those of famous brands which
were registered in Part A (*Chanel* v. *L'Arome*, 1992). In the future the
law may be changed so as to permit a comparison, so long as it is fair.
One of the troubles with this sort of a law is that different people have
different views as to what amounts to fairness. And another is that
companies all too often stretch the comparison too far. The *Compaq*
case is an example of this (see Chap. 14).

To infringe, the mark must be used "in the course of trade," (or for
a service mark, "in connection with the provision of any services")
and must be written or printed: speaking a mark is not infringement,
although it may involve passing-off. Also, the mark must be used in
some sort of trade mark sense. It should be noted, however, that there
will be no infringement unless the registration covers the "wrong"
goods or services; for instance, if "Clippo" were registered for
"three-hole razor-blades imported from Venezuela," it would be an
infringement to label other Venezuelan blades "better than Clippo,"
but it would be no infringement to put the same statement on blades
made in England. This is a typical example of the complications
caused by registering marks too narrowly.

(c) Restricting use by others of a registered trade mark

The owner of a trade mark is allowed in certain cases to extend still
further the rights given him by registration: he may prevent purchasers of goods carrying the mark (unless they remove entirely from

those goods the mark and the maker's name) from altering the packing or get-up of the goods, or the mark or any lettering associated with it. Further, a purchaser may be prevented from using the mark on the goods concerned after their condition has changed or been modified. Thus it would be made an infringement (if the owner of the trade mark wanted) to sell a second-hand or rebuilt type-writer under the original trade mark; or to sell goods loose under the trade mark where they were originally put up in packets; or to remove a trade mark which indicated the quality of a particular line without removing all markings that connect the line with a particular manufacturer. The imposition of this sort of restriction calls for a written agreement covering the actual goods concerned, and is not often done, probably because most mark owners do not know about it. There is no corresponding provision for service marks.

Where the owner of a mark has himself used his mark, or allowed it to be used, for his own goods or services (and provided, in the case of a mark for goods, that there is no such agreement covering the goods) it can never be an infringement to sell them under that mark— although it may amount to passing-off. Thus the multinational Revlon company could not use its United Kingdom registered trade mark to stop the import of the United States Revlon shampoo, even though the UK mark was registered in the name of a subsidiary—the owner had consented to the use, *Revlon*, 1980. On the other hand Colgate could stop the import of genuine South American toothpaste made by the Colgate subsidiary there (*Colgate* v. *Markwell*, 1989). The product was inferior and the public here complained a lot (and what is more many were willing to come to court to give evidence) which is probably why the Court of Appeal found in Colgate UK's favour: it is difficult legally to understand why the case is different from *Revlon*. To use a mark on goods with which the owner has no business connection starts off by being an infringement, of course. But if it is allowed to go on for some time on at least a reasonable scale, the infringer may be able to legitimise his position by obtaining his own registration. If the owner of the mark positively consents to this sort of use his registration will become invalid in most cases (see Chap. 11).

EXCEPTIONS TO THE GENERAL INFRINGEMENT RULES

(a) Accessories and spares

Accessories and spares can, if necessary, be sold by reference to the trade marks used on the goods they are spares or accessories for, provided care is taken not to suggest they are made by or connected with the owners of the marks—there is a difference between "spares for Rover" and "Rover spares"—and provided it is reasonably necessary. Thus in the photographic trade, it is customary and proper to sell accessories, such as lenses, by reference to the brands of camera they fit; there is, after all, no other sensible way of describing them. But film is not normally sold in that sort of way, because only in special cases is it necessary to name the camera: there are standard code numbers which in most cases will give purchasers all the information they need. There are similar provisions for services.

(b) Use of one's own name

Honest use by a trader of his own name, or the name of his place of business, cannot be an infringement of trade or service mark; this applies to companies as well as to individuals. Furthermore, a trader who causes no more confusion than is inseparable from the use of his own name will not be guilty of passing-off. (He may have to avoid putting his name actually on his goods.) But the name must be genuinely his own (his full name, if necessary); and if he uses it to deceive he may be held to be passing-off even though the Act gives him a defence to an action for infringement. Nor may a man who forms a company lend his name to it, so as to give it a special right to use the name.

(c) Honest use as a description

A mark cannot be infringed by an honest description of goods or services, where people reading the description will not think of it as referring to the owner of the mark or his goods. This is not a point that often arises, except with those rare registered trade marks (like "Yale" for locks or "Vaseline" for petroleum jelly) that the public use as the common name for the goods. Obviously, a trader who habitually uses other people's trade marks for his own goods is likely to land in trouble in the end, notwithstanding this provision of the Act; but it covers exceptional cases where a customer needs to have the position explained, and also occasional genuine slips. There will in future probably be similar problems with service marks.

(d) Old established marks

Registration of a mark will not enable its owner to stop anyone who was using it before registration (and has used it ever since) from going on using it, unless the registered owner started using it first. In each case only use on the particular sort of goods or services concerned counts. Suppose for instance, a trade mark is registered by the A Co. for tobacco generally. It later turns out that the B Co. have for some time been using a mark very like it on pipe tobacco. The A Co. can stop the use for pipe tobacco if and only if they or their predecessors in business used their mark on pipe tobacco before the B Co. started using theirs. The A Co. may have been using their mark on cigarettes for the many years, but this is irrelevant. On the other hand, the B Co.'s rights are limited to pipe tobacco; they cannot extend the use of their mark to cover cigarettes, unless they can get it registered for cigarettes (as to which see the next chapter). Such a state of affairs ought, however, never to be allowed to arise; both companies ought to have applied to register their marks earlier; while the B Co. ought to have opposed the A Co.'s application for registration, so as to cut pipe tobacco out of the list of goods covered by it.

WHO SHOULD BE SUED FOR INFRINGEMENT

Most prudent traders avoid the possibility of infringement by checking the Register of trade marks before adopting a new mark. But if infringement does occur, an action to enforce the rights of the owner of the mark may be brought either against the person who applied the mark to the goods in the first place (or imported them, if they were marked abroad), or against anyone who has subsequently traded in them. Each subsequent trader, however, will usually have the right to bring into the action as a "third party" the person who sold the goods to him, so that in the last resort whoever marked or imported the goods will usually be liable for the whole of the damages, and if he has the money to pay them there will often be commercial advantages in bringing the action against him only. Dealers lower down the line are seldom sued unless the owner of the mark cannot discover who made or imported the goods (suing the dealer may be one way of finding this out), or the dealers themselves have large stocks of falsely-marked goods.

In this connection, service marks are ordinarily quite different from trade marks: the trade mark is on the goods, and stays with them as they pass from hand to hand. Service marks are ordinarily used just by the one business that actually provides the services.

CONTESTED ACTIONS

The defendant in an action for infringement of trade mark can (and if he fights the case at all usually does) claim by way of defence that the registration of the mark is invalid, and ask the court to cancel it. The case is likely to be lengthy, complicated and expensive, though not as expensive as a passing-off action would be. If the validity of the registration is disputed and is upheld by the court the owner of the mark may ask the court for a "certificate of validity" for the registration (just as in a patent case, see Chap. 5). In practice, the certificate acts as a warning to the trade that this particular mark is too firmly established to be safely challenged.

SPECIAL RULES FOR PART B MARKS

When a mark is registered in Part B of the register, there is generally no right to sue for infringement if it can be proved that whatever has been done will not confuse or mislead the public. In particular, cases of infringement of the "this is as good as 'Kodak' " type can never occur with "Part B" marks if the statement made is true.

NOTE: TESTS FOR INFRINGEMENT

It is useful to compare the test of whether two marks are too close to one another, for the purpose of infringement of A and B marks, with the standard tests for registrability set out in the next chapter. For an A mark, the test is almost that under section 12: Is there any normal and fair use of the two marks concerned, for the goods or services concerned, that would lead to confusion? Thus "get-up" is irrelevant. For B mark, we look for confusion between any normal and fair use of the plaintiff's (registered) mark, and the actual use the defendant is making of his (allegedly infringing) mark. The test for passing-off is similar to that for B infringement: we consider the actual use the defendant is making of his mark, having regard to the reputation acquired by the plaintiff's mark. (The burden of proof is of course different in these various cases.) Although this is probably what the section of the Act about Part B marks means, the language could have other meanings too (see *Broad* v. *Graham Building Supplies*, 1969).

10

HOW TO REGISTER A MARK

Introduction

THIS chapter explains what sort of thing can be registered as a trade or service mark, gives an outline of the procedure for registration, discusses the conditions for registration to be possible, and explains when other people's applications can be successfully opposed. As before, the bulk of the chapter deals with Part A registrations; Part B registrations are different in ways discussed at the end of the chapter.

What is a "Mark"?

Almost anything changing the appearance of the goods can be a "mark": coloured threads woven into a hose, for instance (*Redaway*, 1914) or even the colouring of pellets inside a part-transparent drug capsule (*Smith Kline & French*, 1975). The one exception, so far, is shapes, of containers and other packages (*Coca Cola*, 1985).

Registrable Marks

To be registrable, a mark must be in use or intended for use as a trade or service mark, and must be distinctive.

(a) Mark must be used as a trade or service mark

A mark is not used as a trade mark, and so is not registrable, unless it is used to indicate a business connection between the owner of the mark and his goods or services. It does not matter what sort of connection; manufacturers, dealers, importers, even people who never own the goods or arrange for others to provide the services, can all have registered marks. In the case of accessories, for instance, the maker of the article they are to be used with may apply a trade mark to them to show he approves their use with his goods; "Kodak Film" might mean (though in fact it does not) film made and sold by an entirely different concern and approved for use with "Kodak" cameras. But there must be some trade connection between the owner of the mark and the goods before they get into the hands of consumers or the actual provision of the services: otherwise, the mark is not used as a trade or service mark. There can be no valid registration of a mark that is never really going to be used at all (*Huggars*, 1979); nor of a picture-mark that merely illustrates the goods and does not point to the owner of the mark at all (*"Striped Toothpaste," Unilever*, 1984). As an extreme example, it was decided that a mark applied by a company whose business was the repairing of stockings, to the stockings they repaired, was not a trade mark and so could not then be registered (*Aristoc* v. *Rysta*, 1945). Such marks are registrable as service marks now.

(b) Marks must be distinctive

The most important requirement for a registrable mark is that it must be distinctive, in the sense of being suitable for distinguishing goods or services with which its owner has some business connection from those of other concerns. (It must also be sufficiently unlike other people's marks for the public not to confuse them; but that is rather a different point and will be discussed later on.) For the purpose of deciding the question of distinctiveness the law divides marks into three sorts: those which will be presumed to be distinctive; those which can never be distinctive; and those which come in between, that is they are refused registration unless it is proved that they have become distinctive in use.

(i) Marks presumed to be distinctive

The most important of these are invented or fanciful words, and designs. These are only refused registration if they are proved to be in common use in the trade concerned or are too like existing marks.

(ii) Marks which can never be distinctive

These are marks that anyone might want to use, such as names of countries or substantial towns; words that are mere laudatory epithets—or words that sound exactly the same as any of these. The clearest case on the point is *Yorkshire Copper Works*, 1954 in which, even though the applicants offered to show that the mark "York-shire" meant their pipe fitting to 100 per cent. of those in the trade, registration was refused, the House of Lords saying that such distinctiveness was merely transient in the sense that another manufacturer might wish to set up a pipe-fitting plant in Yorkshire. More recently, "York" was refused registration for trailers, for the same reason (*York*, 1981). Other cases are "Electrix" (for electric vacuum cleaners—it sounds like "Electrics," *Electrix*, 1959) and "Perfection" (for soap, *Crosfield*, 1909). Further examples are in *Kerly*.

(iii) Marks whose distinctiveness must be proved

In between these extremes comes a large class of marks that are unregistrable when newly adopted, but can become registrable when use over a sufficient period has made them familiar as trade or service marks. When application for registration of such a mark is made, the Registrar has to balance its inherent unsuitability for registration against the evidence produced by the applicant that the mark has become distinctive. How much evidence is needed depends of course on the particular mark; some (very rare surnames, for instance, or the names of obscure foreign towns) may be almost inherently registrable; some (common surnames, larger towns) almost totally unregistrable. Words that come rather close to describing the goods or services come into this category, as well as geographical names and surnames. As an example, the word "Livron" was accepted for registration for use on a medicine containing liver and iron, but it was taken off the register again on the ground that it was the name of a small town in France where another manufacturer of drugs had a factory (*Boots*, 1937). Personal names are in much the same position as surnames alone (although the signature of the applicant for registration or a predecessor in business of his comes into class (i) above). Names of companies must also be proved to be distinctive (unless they are "represented in a special or particular manner," when again they fall into class (i)). Initials are very hard to get registered, because they are shared by many people and companies; only the very best-known companies are allowed to register them (B.P., for instance, and E.M.I.) and even then registration is usually with some sort of pictorial arrangement or "device." Further examples of this "in between" class are "Trakgrip" which was registered for motor tyres on proof that only the applicants used it and that other traders would be unlikely to want to use it to describe their own goods (*Dunlop*, 1942); and "Sheen" for cotton, on evidence of widespread use by the applicants (*J. & P. Coats*, 1936).

(c) Distinctiveness in practice

In all these matters, the fundamental question is: would registration embarrass other traders? Is the matter constituting the mark something that other traders might reasonably want to employ, otherwise than for dishonest purposes, in describing or advertising their goods? If so, it should not be registered; if not, it may be registrable.

When a mark has been used for some time on a large scale, however, a position is likely to arise where it is so well known as one trader's mark that no honest competitor would use it. At that stage, a mark that was unregistrable before comes close to registrability; and in the end, all but the sort of marks we have mentioned as being totally unregistrable will be allowed registration. However, it would seldom be wise for a business to use an unregistrable mark hoping to register it later. The risk of failure is too great, even in those rare cases where there is a good chance of monopolising an existing demand. Most of the cases of attempts at late registration have been cases where trade mark questions were not fully considered when the goodwill was built up; and only too often the attempt has failed. (*The Electrix story*, at the end of Chap. 11, shows how this sort of thing can happen.) Sometimes, though, for a short-lived product, it may make sense to pick a mark too descriptive ever to become registrable during the product's life; the descriptive character of the mark can make it easier for the public to recognise.

THE APPLICATION

Application to register a mark must be made to the Registrar of Trade Marks (except in the case of registrations of trade marks for cotton and metal goods, which can at present, if preferred, be applied for instead in Manchester and Sheffield respectively). The Registrar's office is at the Patent Office, which he administers under the alternative title of Comptroller-General of Patents, Designs and Trade Marks. The office is now in Newport, Wales but it is possible to file documents in London. The office is part of the Department of Trade, which also has certain direct responsibilities in relation to trade marks. Applications are normally made by trade mark agents, who are usually but not always patent agents too. It is wise to employ an experienced agent. Using the services of an agent and given the average sort of problem with the Registry, the costs of obtaining a registration are of the order of £600, of which about half are official fees.

The registration must be renewed (fee currently around £150) after seven years and thereafter every 14 years.

(a) The classes of goods and services

Goods are divided into 34 classes for trade mark purposes, services into another eight, and on those comparatively rare occasions when registration of a mark is wanted for more than one class, separate applications are needed and the resulting registrations are treated as separate. "Registration" in this book will normally mean "registration for a selection of goods or services all in one class." Typical classes of goods are: machines and machine-tools; fuels, industrial oils and lubricants; vehicles; clothing; games and playthings; wines, spirits and liqueurs. The "service" classes are fewer and broader: *e.g.* "Advertising and Business" (such as efficiency-experts and copy-bureaux); or "Material Treatment" (such as "engraving," which could be of jewellery or of tombstones).

In most classes, registrations for all goods in the class will be allowed by the Registrar, and where this is so, that should be the normal form of registration; for reasons, some of which were pointed out in the last chapter, too wide a registration is better than too narrow. The applicant is only entitled, however, to a registration covering those goods and services on which he is using or intends to use the mark, and those "of the same description" (for the meanings of this expression see the beginning of the last chapter). A wider registration than this may be refused by the Registrar, and if obtained may be pruned down later on.

A registration as wide as the whole class, or even covering "goods (or "services") of the same description," may be difficult, for the mark may contain wording that would be misleading if applied to other things in the same class or of the same description: a word suggesting "nylon," for instance, applied to cotton shirts. Yet the owner of the mark must try to cover such cases: for that sort of misleading use would be the most damaging sort of infringement. Similar problems arise with marks implying a particular place of origin (*e.g.* a mark including the Venezuelan flag). Usually, the registrar will allow registration on condition the mark is only used so as not to mislead (as with "Maltesers," registered on condition that the goods it was used on should actually contain malt); if not, it is sometimes possible to get over the difficulty by registering a "series" of marks, alike except for small variations making them suitable for use for the different goods and services or on goods from the different countries concerned. Otherwise, only in exceptional cases should a registration narrower than the "description" be asked for, and even then care should be taken to include spare parts and accessories, or ancillary services.

(b) Who must apply

The application must be made by the person, firm or company actually using or intending to use the mark. If the registration is obtained by someone not intending to use the mark the registration may be invalid, and may remain invalid even if the mark is subsequently handed over to the right owner. Thus, where a mark is in use by a private company on its goods, an application to register it in the name of (say) the chief shareholder would be refused by the Registrar if he knew the true facts; if it were so registered the registration would be invalid, and even if the Registrar could be persuaded to register an assignment to the company the registration might still be invalid. There are, however, two exceptions to this rule. The first is that if the mark is to be used by a company not yet formed, it may be registered by anyone who intends to assign it to the company in due course; but it must be so assigned within 12 months or the registration will be cancelled. The second exception arises in connection with "registered users" and will be referred to in the next chapter. There is a third, unofficial exception, that it does not much matter in whose name a mark is originally registered, provided it gets into the right hands before any use is made of it; but it is much better not to rely on this exception and to register correctly in the first place.

(c) Joint applicants

There may be two or more applicants if and only if they are all going to have a business connection with all the goods or services sold under the mark. For instance, a foreign manufacturer and the sole importer of his goods may register a mark in their joint names; but if some of the goods on which the mark is used are going to be manufactured in this country such a registration will be invalid. If some of the goods are to be made by one manufacturer and some by another a joint registration will almost certainly be invalid. The difficult problem of finding arrangements that can be used in such cases without making the registration invalid is discussed further in the next chapter. Joint registrations, however, should be avoided, unless it is essential for commercial reasons that two independent companies should both retain control over the mark. Their main use may be where services are to be provided by a joint enterprise.

(d) Objections by the Registrar

The Registrar may object to an application on the ground that the mark concerned is inherently not distinctive; may demand evidence or better evidence that it is distinctive; may object that the specification of goods or services that the registration is to cover is too wide; may object that the mark is immoral, illegal, improper, scandalous or misleading; or may object (after searching the register for similar marks) that the mark is too like others on the register or in use. The applicant may meet these objections by withdrawing his application or altering it (changing the specification of goods to be covered, asking for a "Part B" instead of a "Part A" registration and so on), or may demand a "hearing"; that is, the right to go to the Patent Office (or to a special video link set-up in London) and argue the case before the Registrar or one of his senior assistants. The actual arguing, in practice, is done by the agent or by counsel.

If at the hearing the Registrar is not persuaded, the applicant may appeal to the High Court or (if he prefers) to the Board of Trade. Alternatively, the applicant may submit a written case to the Registrar instead of asking for a hearing, and may appeal as before if the Registrar does not change his mind. Appeals to the Board of Trade are referred to Queen's Counsel with special trade mark experience for decision; which is cheaper and quicker.

About half the applications for registration fail altogether. About one in 5 applications for a "Part A" mark, results in a "Part B" registration after argument with the Registrar; that is how most (over 50%.) of "Part B" registrations came about.

These days (things were much worse a few years ago) it takes between six to nine months to obtain a registration if all goes smoothly. Of course if there are objections it may take longer. This emphasises the need to apply for registration well in advance of actual use. (Some businesses even "stockpile" registrations, ready for immediate use when some appropriate product comes up for marketing; but this is probably not supposed to happen, and marks in the stockpile will be vulnerable to attack at least until they are used on a specific product.)

(e) Acceptance and advertisement

If and when the Registrar has no further objection to the mark, the application will be accepted and the intention to register it will be advertised in *The Trade Marks Journal*. If the Registrar is especially doubtful of a mark, or it is the sort of mark that cannot be registered unless it is proved to be distinctive, he may advertise the application (and so ask for oppositions) before accepting it. In either case the mark will not be actually registered until long enough after the advertisement for anyone who wants to oppose the application to do so. The Registrar will allow the applicant and any opponent to argue the case before him if they wish and the loser can appeal to the High Court. If there is no successful opposition, the Registrar will register the mark unless the Board of Trade tells him not to.

(f) Opposition

Anyone may oppose an application, either on the ground that the Registrar ought not to have accepted it or on the ground that the registration would be invalid if it were made. The usual reason for opposition is that the new mark is too similar to a mark the opponents are using or have registered or hope to use or register. (Once they have decided to oppose the application at all, however, opponents will naturally raise any other objections to it that they can find.) For instance, an application to register "Bali" (for brassiéres) was successfully opposed by the owners of "Berlei" (*"Bali,"* 1969), while an application to register "Ovax" was unsuccessfully opposed by the owners of "Hovis" (*"Ovax,"* 1946; see below). Or the owner of a series of marks having a common feature may object to an application by anyone else to register a mark that might look like another member of the series; for instance, a manufacturer wishing to distinguish his goods by the name of the city where they are made, and unable to persuade the Registrar to accept that name as a trade mark, may produce much the same effect by registering a number of marks containing that name ("Bombay Buttercup," "Bombay Bombshell" and so on), and at the same time opposing any application by anyone else to register any mark containing it.

Oppositions are often bitterly fought, not only by opponents (who have often much to lose, since the new registration might reduce the value of their existing goodwill), but also by applicants although (as was pointed out above) the goodwill in a new mark can seldom be worth the legal costs involved. The opposition proceedings may even, in the course of successive appeals, reach the House of Lords, which will involve the loser in costs of at least a hundred thousand pounds and probably a lot more.

(a) The main ground—similarity of marks

The main ground of opposition, that of similarity to existing marks, may be put in two ways: first, that the familiarity of the public with existing marks (registered or unregistered) is such that they would be seriously misled or confused by the use of the mark whose registration is now asked for; and, secondly, that the new mark, and some mark already registered, could be so used by their respective owners (without going outside the terms of their respective registrations) as to confuse or mislead the public. These two objections are by no means the same. The first will not apply if the older mark has not in fact acquired any public reputation and in particular if it has never been used at all. The second will not apply if the older mark is unregistered.

(b) The burden is on the applicant

It is the responsibility of an applicant for registration to satisfy the Registrar that if his mark is registered and used no confusion will arise in either of these two ways. If he cannot so satisfy the Registrar (or the court on appeal from the Registrar), his application will fail.

The Registrar will sometimes accept an application, where the only objection is the existence on the register of a similar mark whose owner consents to the new application; but this will only be done in cases where no serious confusion is to be expected. The advertisement of such an application will state that it is made "by consent."

If there are other similar marks on the register belonging to the applicant, this will, of course, be no objection to registration, but the new mark will be "associated" with the old ones; the main effect of this is that they can never belong to different owners, unless the Registrar cancels the association.

(c) The "Ovax" Case

"*Ovax*" (*Smith, Hayden*, 1946) illustrates these points. "Hovis" had been registered since 1895 for "Substances used as food or as ingredients in food," and had been used on a very large scale though apparently only on flour and bread. Hovis Ltd., the proprietors of "Hovis," also owned a mark "Ovi" registered for much the same variety of goods, but there was no evidence that this mark had ever been used at all. The case concerned an application (opposed by Hovis Ltd.) to register the mark "Ovax" for "A cereal preparation for use as an improver and moistening agent in making cakes." The Registrar allowed the application and Hovis Ltd. appealed to the court. Here is the test the court had to apply—as slightly altered by the House of Lords (*Bali*, 1969):

"In these circumstances, the questions for my decision under the two sections of the Act have been formulated, and I think accurately formulated, as follows: (a) (under section 11) 'Having regard to the use of the name "Hovis," is the court satisfied that the mark applied for, if used in a normal and fair manner in connection with any goods covered by the registration proposed, will not be reasonably likely to cause deception and confusion amongst a substantial number of persons?'; (b) (under section 12) 'Assuming user by Hovis Ltd. of their marks "Hovis" and "Ovi" in a normal and fair manner for any of the goods covered by the registrations of those marks (and including particularly goods also covered by the proposed registration of the mark "Ovax") is the court satisfied that there will be no reasonable likelihood of deception or confusion among a substantial number of persons if Smith, Hayden & Co. Ltd. also use their mark "Ovax" normally and fairly in respect of any goods covered by their proposed registration?'
It is clear that the onus lies upon Smith, Hayden & Co. Ltd., as applicants for registration, of satisfying the court that a negative answer should be given to both questions, regard being had to the range of goods covered by the proposed registration."

It will be seen that the second question covers a wider field of inquiry than the first, so that if the second can be answered "Yes," the first need seldom be asked.

In the "*Ovax*" case, the court was satisfied that there was no such likelihood of confusion or deception and allowed "Ovax" to be registered.

(d) Other examples

In *Jellinek*, 1946 the applicant sought to register for shoe polish a mark containing the word "Panda" and a panda's picture, and was opposed by the owners of a mark registered for boots and shoes and containing the word "Panda" with a different picture of a panda. The opposition was based on both the grounds explained above. It failed on the first ground, because the opponents had not yet actually used their mark at the time when the applicants applied for theirs, so that there was no reputation among the public which could make use of the new mark misleading. It failed on the second ground because the court held that shoes and shoe polish are not goods "of the same description" (that is, they belong to two different trades: see the beginning of the last chapter); and when this is so, the second ground of objection does not apply. Again, an application to register "Jardex" for disinfectants was opposed by the owners of a registration of "Jardox" for an extract of meat: *Edward*, 1946. The second ground of objection did not arise (since meat extract and disinfectant are not goods of the same description), but the opponents' meat extract had been sold to hospitals on a considerable scale and the applicants' disinfectant was poisonous and, in view of the disastrous consequences that might result from confusion in a hospital between the two products the application was rejected on the first ground. The Registrar also pointed out that it was his duty, under the general discretion he possesses to refuse all objectionable trade mark applications, to refuse to register any mark whose use might so endanger the public.

REGISTRATION IN CASES WHERE CONFUSION IS LIKELY

In special circumstances, a mark may be registered notwithstanding a likelihood of confusion. In such cases the Registrar may impose limitations on registration or conditions on use, so as to minimise the danger of misleading the public. For instance, a mark might be registered for goods to be exported only, or only for goods to be sold or services provided in particular areas in this country. In *Bass* v. *Nicholson*, 1932 there was an application to register for bitter beer a mark including a triangle; the application was opposed by Bass, who had a very well-known trade mark for pale ale and beer consisting of a triangle, usually but by no means always used in the form of a red triangle. The Registrar allowed the application, but only for a white triangle (white being the only colour the applicants had used); the case ultimately reached the House of Lords, who upheld this decision but further limited the registration by excluding bottled beer from it.

Where a confusing mark is registered because of special circumstances, the Registrar has special powers further to reduce the danger of confusion by limiting the registrations of marks already registered so as to prevent their use on goods or in areas where they are not already used. These powers to cut down existing registrations are discussed in the next chapter.

The "special circumstance" usually relied on as justifying the presence on the register of two conflicting marks is what is called "honest concurrent use": that the mark whose registration is now asked for has been in actual use for some years. In the *"Triangle"* case, for instance, the applicants had been using their mark since before the Trade Marks Register was opened. The mark has to have been used honestly, and less than some seven years of reasonably large-scale use is unlikely to justify registration.

MORE ABOUT CONFUSION

The insistence on avoiding any likelihood of confusing or misleading the public runs through the whole of trade mark law. The confusion that may arise from the simultaneous use of two similar marks is only one instance. Another instance occurred when "Orwoola" was registered as a trade mark for various articles including clothing. The Court of Appeal had to decide whether it ought to remain registered. Lord Justice Fletcher Moulton said:

> "This case presents no difficulty. It is in substance a case of registration of the word 'All wool,' grotesquely mis-spelt, as a trade mark for textile fabrics. ... If the goods are made wholly of wool, the words are natural and almost necessary description of them. If they are not made wholly of wool it is a mis-description that is so certain to deceive that its use can hardly be otherwise than fraudulent. In either case the words are utterly unfit for registration as a trade mark": (*"Orlwoola,"* 1909)

REMOVAL FROM THE REGISTER

After a mark has been registered, it can be removed, either by application to the Registrar with appeal to the court or by direct application to the court in two broad classes of case, namely where there was something wrong with the original registration and where something has gone wrong after registration. In theory the original registration of a "Part B" mark always remains open to attack, but the original registration of "Part A" marks is protected to a certain degree after seven years: see below.

It is harder to get a mark taken off the register than to prevent its registration; if there is any doubt about the case no action will be taken, so that an unregistered mark will stay off the register and a registered mark will stay on. Furthermore, if the objections to registration have gone in the meantime—for example, if a mark that was not distinctive has since become so—the court will probably refuse to strike the mark off.

The classes of case where a mark can be removed for post-registration defects are limited to those set out in the Act; there is no general removal power ("*GE*," 1973). These cases are more fully discussed in the next chapter. They consist of non-use, deceptiveness arising through the fault of the proprietor, and certain types of descriptiveness.

When the mark has been registered in Part A for seven years, the question whether it ought to have been registered in the first place can only be reopened if registration was obtained by fraud; or if the mark was illegal, immoral, improper or scandalous; or if use of the mark would be likely to confuse or mislead the public by reason of previous use of some similar mark, not merely by reason of the presence of a similar mark on the register. This last ground can be important; but in general a seven-year-old "Part A" registration is safe enough provided its owner uses it and avoids the pitfalls discussed in the next chapter.

DEFENSIVE REGISTRATION OF TRADE MARKS

The law does not discourage the use of similar trade marks by firms in quite different trades; it has already been pointed out that a mark cannot be validly registered in the ordinary way so as to cover goods belonging to a different trade from that in which the mark is actually to be used. (It is quite hard enough nowadays to find a satisfactory trade mark without worrying about marks used in other trades.) Some trade marks, however, are so well known that members of the public seeing them on quite different goods would be likely to suppose that those goods were connected with the company that normally used the mark. Trade marks of this sort, if and only if the mark consists of "an invented word or words," may be "defensively" registered for any goods to which their reputation extends in this way; but getting such registrations is not easy, the registration will for technical reasons be less valuable than an ordinary one, and as a result such registrations are very rare. It normally makes more sense just to get an ordinary registration. There is no provision for defensive registration of service marks.

"Part B" Marks

The rules for applications to register trade marks in Part B of the register are the same as for Part A, except that the standard of distinctiveness is lower. A "Part B" mark need not be distinctive when registered, so long as it is capable of becoming distinctive in use. So "Ustikon" has been registered for stick-on rubber soles: *Davis* v. *Sussex Rubber*, 1927. Marks such as "Yorkshire," that are totally unregistrable in Part A, are not registrable in Part B either: for they can never become truly distinctive. In theory, indeed, with any mark that can be registered only upon exceptionally strong evidence that it has become distinctive, there ought seldom to be a case where the evidence justifies registration in Part B without equally justifying registration in Part A. Where there is an objection to registration on the ground of closeness to an existing mark, too, it is theoretically little easier to get a B than an A registration. In practice, however, it seems that a mark that for any reason is just on the borderline of registrability in Part A will usually be accepted by the Registrar for Part B. This is what Part B is for.

There is a type of mark which is registrable in Part B, but not later in Part A even when it is wholly distinctive, "*Weldmesh*," 1966. But not even lawyers can understand what the limits of this class are, and most Part B marks can be reregistered in Part A after proof of use to a considerable extent. As soon as this is the case the owner of the mark can, and normally should, make a fresh application to register it, this time in Part A. Not only does the change give the owner greater rights to stop infringement and simplify the bringing of infringement actions, it also helps to make his ownership more secure; for the rule protecting seven-year-old registrations does not apply to "Part B" marks.

There is one purpose for which a "Part B" registration is as good as any other. Some countries require trade marks registered for use by British firms to have been previously registered here, but do not distinguish between the two parts of our register. This was the main reason why Part B was established, and it is a pity that registration in Part B was so narrowly restricted. There is a need for a Part C, containing a mere record of actual marks in use, so as to enable foreign registrations to be based on them.

In any case, a "Part B" registration is much better than no registration at all.

11

PITFALLS IN TRADE MARK LAW

INTRODUCTION

THE purpose of this chapter is to explain what precautions should be taken to keep a trade mark registration valid. It applies both to "Part A" and to "Part B" marks.

The law on this subject is not in a satisfactory state. It was recognised before 1938 that the technicalities of the law made it sometimes very difficult to preserve the validity of trade marks, and the 1938 Act included important changes intended to make preservation easier. But even now the effect of the Act is by no means clear, so that it is not always safe to assume that the old difficulties have gone. Furthermore, some other countries remain more rigid in outlook, so that marks used on some exported goods have to be handled according to the old rules. By and large, in most countries, it is possible somehow or other to do anything with a trade mark that can be done here, but there are exceptions.

THE OLD RULE:—THE MARK MUST NOT MISLEAD

The basic rule of the old law was that a trade mark must never be allowed to be misleading. It followed that the owner of a mark must never allow anyone else to use it; for it ought to be associated in the public mind with his goods only, and if it were used on anyone else's goods this must mislead the public either as to whose goods they were or as to who was the owner of the mark. It followed, also, that a mark could never be transferred from one owner to another except together with the whole goodwill of the business in which it was used; for the mark ought to be associated in the public mind with that business, so that any use of it by a new owner must be misleading. If the business was split up or came to an end, its trade marks were considered to be abandoned. Nor could the owner of a trade mark change the nature of his trade connection with the goods it was used on; if, for instance, the mark belonged to a manufacturer, and he started using it on goods made by someone else and merely distributed by him, the public would think he was still the manufacturer and so be misled. In this country these subsidiary rules have been largely abolished by the 1938 Act; but the mark will be invalid either if it was likely to deceive or cause confusion at the time when it was registered or if it has become likely to cause confusion since the date by reason of some blameworthy act of the registered proprietor ("*GE*" 1973).

CHANGING THE WAY THE MARK IS USED

Consider, for instance, a change in type of trade connection, and consider as an example the manufacturer who starts using his mark on goods made for him by someone else. The 1938 Act says that such a change in the way the mark is used is not to be considered as sufficient in itself to make the mark misleading. The difficulty arises if the public are in fact misled—if they do in fact believe that the marked goods are still made by the same people. Does this make the registration of the mark invalid? Probably not, but there is no certainty about it. The only really safe course is to advertise widely the nature of the new arrangements; but few proprietors do.

CHANGE IN OWNERSHIP

Where the mark is transferred to a new owner the law is clearer. If the mark is in use, and the goodwill in the business is not transferred together with the mark, the new owner must apply to the Registrar for directions within six months, and must then advertise the change of ownership in the way the Registrar directs. When he has done this (but not until then), the transfer of the mark will be valid so far as this country goes (although it is not clear whether the transfer then has retrospective effect back to the date when it was actually made); and if the mark was valid before the transfer it will almost (but not quite) certainly be valid in this country afterwards. If there is any doubt whether enough goodwill has been transferred with the mark to satisfy the old rules, it will always be safer to ask for the Registrar's direction: if he does not demand any advertisements, so much the better. An unregistered mark used in the same business as a registered mark may be transferred together with it, and subject to the same rules. Otherwise, unregistered marks may only be transferred under the stricter rules of the older law.

If a mark has been registered in the wrong name (for instance, in the name of a shareholder or a director of the company that uses it), a transfer of this sort into the right name will almost certainly be a valid transfer. Whether the registration as a whole is valid will then depend on whether the mark can be attacked as having been wrongly registered in the first place. If the only thing wrong with the registration was the owner's name, the position will then be as follows. If the mark was in use when it was registered, it may have been misleading at the time of registration; it will in that case be vulnerable, although the court will probably refuse to strike it off the register once it is no longer misleading. If the mark was not in use when it was registered, it will now be valid. Such transfers are unpopular with the Registrar, who prefers to avoid all legal technicalities by demanding a fresh application to register in the new name followed by cancellation of the old registration. This course, however, involves a loss in seniority that should not be accepted if a transfer will make the registration valid.

SPLIT OWNERSHIP

Transfers that will result in the ownership of a mark, or of similar marks that are too much alike, being split among two or more proprietors are still not allowed. If there is doubt as to the legitimacy of a transfer, the Registrar may be asked to certify that it is valid; his certificate, if the facts are put to him fairly, will settle the matter once and for all. (But the mark may still become invalid if in fact the public is confused by the two new owners.) Transfers that give one owner the use of the mark for export and another the use of it in this country are valid so far as our law is concerned; transfers that give the mark to different owners for different parts of the United Kingdom are not legitimate unless specially approved by the Registrar. A mark can be transferred for some only of the goods or services it is registered for, but a transfer leaving things "of the same description" or "associated" goods and services in separately owned registrations counts as a "splitting" transfer.

The transfers referred to in the last paragraph have to be entered on the register promptly; other transfers apparently need never be registered at all, but there are technicalities which make it important in practice that they should be.

Apart from these rules about splitting, a mark that has not been used can now be transferred quite freely, so far as this country is concerned. No reference to the Registrar is necessary, except afterwards for the purpose of registering the new owner.

PARALLEL IMPORTS

There is inevitably conflict between the right of the owner of a trade mark to decide how and by whom his mark shall be used in any given area, and the ideal of free flow of goods that is fundamental to the European Common Market. By and large, EC principles prevail. Anyone who has allowed goods to be sold in one EC country cannot, whether by trade marks, patents or any other restrictions, prevent their resale in the others. Even though the marks in the two countries are in different ownership, if they had a common origin divided by consent (not by compulsion)—the two owners were once associated concerns, for instance—movement within the EC from one to the other has to be allowed (*Centrafarm* v. *Winthrop*, 1974) (see Chap. 24). An agreement between the two owners, to keep out of each other's preserves, will be invalid as tending to restrict competition and free flow of goods, even if there is no other connection at all between them (*Sirdar's Agreement*, 1975).

The EC's special rules do not apply to goods coming in from outside the EC; but goods that are "genuine" goods, marked by the authority of the owner of the mark, will not normally infringe wherever they come from (see Chap. 24).

LICENSING OF TRADE AND SERVICE MARKS

The law is uncertain

In these days, a good deal of licensing of trade marks goes on; that is, the owner lets other people use his mark, more or less under his control, and may take payment for the privilege. Before 1938, this sort of thing invalidated any registration; since 1938, it is allowable to some extent, but we still do not quite know to what extent. What the 1938 Act actually says, is that in certain circumstances a trader may be registered as a "user" of someone else's mark, and that use of the mark by a registered user counts in law as use by the owner. That is probably the safer way to go about things. But the tendency of some recent decisions is to say that so long as the arrangement could have been the subject of a registration of a user, it does not matter that the registration was never secured.

Registration of users

What the Act provides is that where a user registration is wanted, both parties—owner and user—must apply to the Registrar and show him the arrangement between them. He has a wide discretion whether to register the user or not, but he normally will, so long as the agreement gives the owner some sort of continuing control over the way the mark will be used, so that there is at least the possibility of its remaining under a single control. (It has never been decided, whether the mark becomes invalid if no control is ever exercised; nor whether it matters to what extent the public appreciate what is going on.) In particular, the Registrar recognises as adequate three sorts of control: that of a holding company over its subsidiaries; that given by a contract entitling the owner of the mark to control the quality, etc., of the goods; and that of a patentee over licensees of his patent. In the first case, the marks do not have to be registered in the name of the holding company (although things are tidier that way); in the second and third cases the control can be distinctly unreal.

Character merchandising

It is common in these days for the goodwill created by a successful TV programme or the like to be exploited by "character merchandising": that is, by selling the right to use the names of characters from the series as a sort of trade mark for various sorts of goods. (These are not really trade marks.) The obvious way to do this is by registering the character name as a trade mark for all likely goods, and selling the right to become a registered user for particular goods. But our law does not allow registration to be used for this purpose: it is called "trafficking in the mark" and if the Registrar sees what is going on he will refuse registration (*Holly Hobbie*, 1984).

Licensing of trade marks used for export

Registered users are not recognised by all foreign countries. In any case, registration of a user in this country cannot of itself give the user rights in countries abroad. If, therefore, both the owner and a user, or two users (registered or not), export goods to the same foreign country, proper arrangements, complying with local rules, ought to be made there; otherwise, the mark may become invalid there. This point needs watching, but the difficulty can usually be overcome; for instance, by passing all the exports of the group through a single company, and transferring to that company the right to use all marks for export together with the whole goodwill in the group's export business.

MARKS THAT ARE THE NAME OF THE ARTICLE

Some registered trade marks are habitually used by the general public as the name of the article or substance they are chiefly used on. Typical examples are "Thermos"; "Xerox" copy; "Yale" lock; "Hoover"; and "Biro." Such a habit of the public is of great commercial value to the owners of the marks in this class, but from the legal point of view it raises serious difficulties. On the one hand, no mark can be registered for any goods it describes, for if it is descriptive it cannot be distinctive; at the same time, however, a valid registration cannot become invalid simply because the mark is treated by the general public as describing the goods it is used on. Thus, "Shredded Wheat" was removed from the register, because at the time when it was registered it was simply the description of the breakfast food sold under that trade mark (*Shredded Wheat Co.* v. *Kellogg* 1939) while on the other hand, the registered trade mark "Thermos" cannot become invalid simply because the general public may call any vacuum-flask a "thermos." (This is another advantage of registering marks correctly as soon as it is decided to use them.) If, however, there is a "well-known and established use" of the trade mark, as the name or description of an article, not just by the public but by people trading in the article concerned, the registration will be invalid (unless the use of the mark is confined to the goods of the owner of that mark). Further, such a use in relation to "goods of the same description" is enough to invalidate the mark. Thus, the mark "Daiquiri Rum" had been registered for rum since 1922, but it was removed from the register upon proof that (to persons in the trade) a particular type of cocktail which contained rum, was known as a "Daiquiri cocktail" ("*Daiquiri Rum*" 1969).

An ingenious and malicious dealer, by using this rule, could with a little patience and at some risk of an infringement action being brought against him invalidate almost any trade mark that consists of words. In the case of a mark that is already used by the general public as the name of an article or substance, the job of "breaking" the mark should be quite easy. This is not a serious risk (dealers are not normally malicious, though a rival manufacturer might be); but carelessness on the part of the owners of such marks is. The owners of marks of this type need to keep a careful watch on the language used by members of the trade (on trade journals and dictionaries, especially) to see that careless use of the registered words does not become a habit. Education of the public as well, by suitable choice of advertising methods, to consider the trade mark as a brand name only, will reduce the risk of invalidity. Since, however, it is use by traders that matters from the legal point of view, not use by the public, the state of affairs to be aimed at is one where the trade treat the mark quite strictly as a brand name only while the general public think of it as the name of the article concerned and always ask for that article under the trade mark. In this way legal security can be combined with profitable exploitation of the mark. But an extremely careful watch on the trade will then be essential. Even a most scrupulous trader may fail to appreciate that expressions like "Yale type" are improper. There are similar rules for service marks that will call for care from now on.

There are special rules limiting trade mark registrations for the names of chemical compounds and the names of articles for which there were patents that have recently run out. It has been held, too, that the official names of plant varieties cannot be trade marks.

NON-USE

(a) Removal of disused marks

If a mark is left unused for five years it can be expunged, unless its owner is in a position to show that at some time during those five years he would have used it if he had not been prevented from doing so by "special circumstances" in the trade concerned. The "special circumstances" must affect the trade as a whole, not merely the particular company that owns the marks.

The five years that matter are up to one month before the legal proceedings start; this gives time for the parties to negotiate, if they hurry, without prejudicing the legal position.

"Use" can be by advertisements, *e.g.* in preparation for bringing out a new line; or it may be on samples imported from overseas; any sort of business use will do; possibly even advertisements saying "You cannot buy '—' because there isn't any." But in that sort of case there are probably "special circumstances" explaining why there isn't any.

Where one owner has two marks which are too alike to be both registrable if they belonged to different owners and are consequently registered as "associated marks," the tribunal may (and if the one mark contains the other must) accept use of one as a defence to proceedings based on non-use of the other.

(b) Limitation to things actually used

Where a mark has been used during the past five years for some only of the goods or services covered by the registration, there can be an application to limit the registration by excluding things on which the mark has not been used. So where a company had registered marks containing the word "Columbia" for a large variety of goods including both gramophone records and films, and had used it for gramophone records but not for films, the court cut down the registration to exclude films (*Columbia Graphophone*, 1932). The cutting-down was done at the request of a company which wanted itself to use a "Columbia" mark on cinema films. So far as sound-films were concerned, the court accepted the fact that sound-films had not been invented as a "special circumstance" justifying failure to use the trade on them.

It follows that a registration that is noticeably wider than the description of goods or services on which the mark is actually in use may be of limited value in a dispute, though it will often serve to prevent disputes by warning off competitors who might otherwise be inclined to select new marks uncomfortably close to the old one.

"Ghost marks": A cautionary tale

Two tobacco companies, one British the other American, both wanted the name "Merit" for brands of cigarette. But "Merit," as a "mere laudatory epithet," would certainly be refused registration for lack of distinctiveness. So the British company, to preserve the position for a future launch of "Merit," registered what it called a "ghost mark": a mark not really intended to to be used, but close enough to the real trade mark to conflict with it. They chose "Nerit." They actually sold a few cigarettes labelled "Nerit"—a million or so—so as not to leave the mark totally unused. But the court held that this was not genuine use, and that "Nerit" was never a real trade mark at all. So far so good, but the court went on to say that a mark is not a trade mark unless the goods it is used on are to be sold at a profit (which could disqualify almost anybody, these days) and that "Nerit" and "Merit" are not confusingly similar (which must be wrong): hard cases make bad law.

THE NEED FOR VIGILANCE

If the owner of a registered mark allows a mark like it to be used by the trade as a whole it will probably become descriptive or misleading and so invalid; if he allows a competitor to use such a mark, he will seriously endanger his rights. The sequence of events may for a trade mark be as follows: Suppose that A is the owner of a trade mark for certain goods in Class 34 ("Tobacco, raw or manufactured; smokers' articles; matches"). Suppose he has used his mark on pipe tobacco only, and that this particular brand of tobacco is hardly sold outside Devon and Cornwall. Suppose B now starts using a similar mark on cigarettes in a different part of the country—Lancashire, say. B's mark will at first be unregistrable: it will be too close to A's: cigarettes and pipe tobacco are goods "of the same description"; it has already been assumed that the two marks are alike, and it follows that the new mark cannot be accepted by the Registrar while the old one remains registered. In a few years' time, however, B can come to the Registrar claiming that special circumstances now justify registration. If he succeeds in showing that over a considerable area of the country the mark is now distinctive of his goods and not A's, not only may he be allowed to register his mark (at least for cigarettes sold in Lancashire), but further, once his right to registration has been acknowledged by the Registrar, he can demand that A's registration should be cut down to exclude cigarettes. In due course B, if his cigarettes have a wide sale and he is not stopped, may capture the mark entirely.

Such cases illustrate the danger (insisted on in Chap. 9) of too narrow registration of a mark. For if A has registered his mark for "pipe tobacco" only, he will be unable to stop B from using a similar mark on cigarettes, so long as no passing-off occurs—and in the example suggested there would be little chance of this. If, on the other hand, his registration covers all forms of tobacco, he will be entitled to stop B at the start; for B will infringe his registration, and infringement will continue until B's own mark is registered. But A must use his rights; he must look out for encroachments on his mark and put a stop to them as soon as possible. If he is not sufficiently vigilant, he may find that those rights have ceased to exist.

FOREIGN MARKS

The basic principle of our trade mark law is that the right to registration of a mark depends entirely on distinctiveness in this country.

There is, in principle, no such thing as ownership of an unregistered mark except the sort of ownership that comes from having a goodwill in the mark. This leaves our law in some difficulty, in cases where a British trader registers a mark that belongs to somebody else abroad. Quite apart from the problem of "parallel imports," discussed above, our courts seem fairly determined to stop any deliberate appropriation of other people's marks even where they have no sort of reputation here; but there is no real agreement as to how this is to be done. In at least one case, the court has said that a trader who knows that the mark he seeks to register belongs to some foreign firm cannot (as the Act requires of an applicant for registration) "claim to be the proprietor" of the mark. In another case, a trader made a practice of registering as trade marks for toys and the like the names of characters in American television series that might someday reach this country: if the character appeared on British television, he then exploited the mark. The court said that he did not really mean to use the marks at the time of the applications, and so the marks ought to be struck off. Neither answer seems satisfactory in law.

The "Electrix" Story

To end this chapter on pitfalls, here is a second cautionary tale; the reader may draw the moral for himself. In 1928, or thereabouts, the owners of the trade mark "Electrolux" (for vacuum cleaners and the like) decided to protect their mark by registering "Electrux"; but they did not use "Electrux." In about 1936, another manufacturer started selling vacuum cleaners under the mark "Electrix." The war interfered, but by 1947 both "Electrolux" and "Electrix" were in use on a large scale; "Electrux" was still not being used. The owners of "Electrolux," provoked (it would seem) by a model called "Electrix-de-luxe," decided that "Electrix" must be stopped. Since, however, "Electrux," which was the mark they would have mainly to rely on, had never been used, it was no good suing for infringement since "Electrux" would merely have been struck off. So they had to set to, to use that mark (hurriedly, and quietly lest the "Electrix" people notice the use and apply to strike the mark off before the month was up). So they named a new model the "Electrux." Unfortunately, this model proved unsatisfactory and had to be withdrawn, and conditions being what they were in 1947, it was some time before use could begin again. By the time that "Electrux" could be said to be firmly in use, sales of "Electrix" cleaners had grown still more. What with this and the years that had elapsed since "Electrix" first came into use, it is not surprising that the court seems to have felt some sympathy with "Electrix"; when in due course an action for infringement was started, the court held "Electrix" to be an infringement of "Electrux," but refused to grant an injunction stopping the use of "Electrix" then and there: this was clearly a case where "Electrix" should be allowed first to go away and try to register their mark. If they got registration (and they had nearly 20 years' use to rely on, by that time, some of it on a very large scale), they would have a statutory defence to the action for infringement and that would be that. So the defendants went away and tried to get "Electrix" registered. Everyone agreed, that the length and scale of their use were amply sufficient to justify registration, so far as any objection based on similarity to the mark "Electrux" was concerned. Unfortunately, however "Electrix" sounds the same as "electrics" which means that where electrical goods are concerned it is one of the totally unregistrable marks.

The cases are *Electrolux* v. *Electrix*, 1953 (the infringement action, in the Court of Appeal, where it stopped); *Electrix's Application*, 1959 (in the House of Lords, the application to register "Electrix").

12

CERTIFICATION TRADE MARKS

THE NATURE OF CERTIFICATION TRADE MARKS

THIS chapter is concerned with a special sort of trade mark intended not to indicate the existence of a trade connection between its owner and the goods it is used on, but to indicate that its owner has certified the goods as reaching certain standards. There is no corresponding provision for service marks.

These "certification trade marks," as they are called, only superficially resemble ordinary trade marks. They are not really private property at all. Their owners (who are not allowed to be people trading in the goods concerned) must allow them to be used by any trader whose goods reach the required standards; anyone who is denied the right to use such a mark may appeal to the Registrar. Strictly speaking, this right of appeal will only exist if the "Regulations" for the mark say so; but they are unlikely to be approved if they do not. In the same way, it will be an infringement of a certification mark to apply it to sub-standard goods whether the owner has given permission or not. Before the mark can be registered a set of regulations governing the way the mark is to be used and the standards the marked goods are to comply with, must be approved by the Department of Trade. So long as the mark remains registered the regulations can be inspected at the Patent Office.

The standards may relate to "origin, material, mode of manufacture, quality, accuracy, or other characteristic"—*i.e.* any sort of standard will do provided the Board of Trade can be persuaded to take it seriously. A typical certification mark is that for "hand-woven Harris Tweed"; less typical, perhaps, are the "kite marks" of the British Standards Institution.

APPLICATION

The procedure for registering a certification mark is much the same as for ordinary marks, except that the Registrar cannot accept the application unless the Board of Trade is satisfied that the applicant is competent to certify the goods concerned, that the regulations are satisfactory, and the registration will be to the public advantage. Oppositions to registration by other people can be two-fold: oppositions heard by the Registrar, on the ordinary grounds mentioned in Chapter 10, and oppositions heard by the Board of Trade, on the ground that the Board ought not to have allowed the Registrar to accept the application. In the same way, after the mark has been registered, its validity may be attacked before a court of the Registrar as if it were an ordinary trade mark, or the Board may be asked to cancel it either on the ground that its existence is no longer to the public advantage or on the ground that the proprietor is no longer competent to certify the goods concerned or has failed to comply with the regulations. The Board can also be asked to alter the regulations. It is not unknown, for instance, for regulations to be framed so as to confine use of the mark to the owner's friends. Outsiders might then well object.

In practice the certification trade mark system works without many disputes: one of the two reported cases is *"Stilton" T.M.*, 1967 where the court allowed the mark "Stilton" to be registered for cheese manufactured by members of the Stilton Cheese Makers' Association, whose rules provided that membership was open to any cheese manufacturer in the counties of Leicester, Derby or Nottingham who agreed to manufacture "Stilton" cheese in accordance with the Association's special recipe. In the other reported case a breach of the regulations concerning certification was found not to be serious enough to justify cancellation of the mark (*Sea Island Cotton*, 1989).

INFRINGEMENT

Certification marks are registered in Part A only. They must be distinctive in the same way as other "Part A" marks, and will normally include an indication that they are certification marks. Infringers can be sued in the same way as infringers of any other "Part A" mark; the rules deciding what will be an infringement and what will not are much the same. It is unlikely, however, that the Registrar or the

Board of Trade would allow a certification mark to be registered except for the actual goods it is to be used on, and there is no provision for defensive registration, so that the right to sue infringers will usually be somewhat limited. Any use of such a mark on the wrong goods, however, would be likely to be an offence under the Trade Descriptions Act 1968; this is discussed in Chapter 15.

OTHER FEATURES OF THE SYSTEM

Certification marks cannot change ownership without the permission of the Board of Trade, but there are no other restrictions on changes of ownership. In practice, owners will usually be trade associations or other non-profit-making bodies. The regulations can provide for the owner's own officers to inspect the goods and apply the mark to them; but this is unusual. The usual arrangement is for manufacturers to be authorised to apply the mark to their own goods, under proper control by the owner of the mark. The authorised users of the mark are not registered as users on the Register of Trade Marks; instead, the owners of the mark keep their own register.

A certification mark cannot be removed by the court or the Registrar for non-use (indeed, the court has very little authority over certification marks at all) but the Board would probably be ready in most cases to order unused marks to be taken off the register.

13

THE LAW OF PASSING-OFF

A General Rule

THE general rule governing passing-off is that no trader may so conduct his business so as to lead customers to mistake his goods, or his business, for the goods or business of someone else. The present chapter discusses this rule its ramifications and some partial exceptions to it.

Varieties of Passing-off

Our law lumps together under the name "passing-off" a considerable variety of activities, ranging from simple cases of dishonest trading—where a garage-owner is asked for a particular brand of oil, or a doctor prescribes a particular manufacturer's drug, and the customer is simply given a different and cheaper brand—to cases that are almost cases of infringement of trade mark. In these days, the simple cases are rare; the trades mentioned are unusual in that customers still expect to get something not in the manufacturer's own package. In most shops, goods pretending to be of national brand but supplied unmarked would be immediately suspect. Such things can happen, of course, even if the goods are properly marked—see *Procea* v. *Evans* 1951; and there are more sophisticated versions now and again, such as the manufacturer who declares, untruthfully, that his is the brand you find advertised on television. Or there is the practice of some large supermarket chains of getting up their "own brand" to look like the brand leader's packaging. Whether this is passing-off is yet to be decided at a full hearing, the plaintiff would have to show that the public believed the goods were made for the supermarket by him; the supermarket would say that it used the get-up to indicate honestly that the goods were of the same type and quality as the leading brand. Often the brand leader does not dare sue the supermarket because of the latter's buying power, this is probably why there has never yet been a full trial of the point. There are odd cases too, that fit no general category, but where the court feels that some kind of deceptive conduct ought to be stopped. Whenever one trader manages to benefit from another's goodwill there is likely to be at least an arguable case of passing-off. By and large, though, cases of passing-off are akin to infringements of trade mark, but are cases that do not quite fit into the scheme of the Trade Marks Act.

"BADGES" AND REPUTATIONS

Most cases of passing-off, then, are cases where a trader without in so many words saying that his goods are someone else's nevertheless indicates this by applying to his goods some badge or sign that people have come to regard as a mark of that other's goods. In the simplest case, this badge may be an ordinary trade mark—perhaps a trade mark that for one reason or another is not registered for the goods concerned. (If it is so registered, there will be an infringement as well as passing-off.) It may be the name of a business, or of someone associated with the business. It may be a special appearance or "get-up" of the goods: a specially shaped package, for instance, such as a plastic lemon. But all such cases have these essentials in common: the "badge," whatever it may be, must be one that has come by use in this country to distinguish the goods of a particular trader or group of traders; and it must have been copied, whether deliberately or by accident, closely enough for people to be deceived, or at least to be confused. So the plaintiff in an action to stop the passing-off must prove two things: that the mark or other "badge" he is relying on has a sufficient reputation amongst customers; and that there is a real risk that what the defendant is doing will lead to deception or confusion of those customers. Actually there is also a third thing the plaintiff ought to prove: that the deception causes the customers to buy the wrong brand, though this is often assumed or overlooked, see the discussion in Chapter 7 about using passing-off to protect designs and the *Plastic Lemon* case (below).

The risk of deception

Judging the risk of confusion in these cases is not unlike judging whether one of two trade marks infringes another (a matter we have already discussed). But in a passing-off action, the question is not whether any fair use of the defendant's mark or other "badge" would be likely to cause confusion, but whether what the defendant is actually doing is misleading, so that a court may have to look at all the circumstances to see whether they increase or decrease the risk. It may be important, for instance, whether and how the defendant puts his own name on his goods, and what if anything his name will mean to the customer. It may also be important to what extent the customers already know where the goods come from. A business dealing direct with manufacturers probably knows very well whom it is buying from, and is unlikely to be confused by misleading markings; it is when the goods get into shops that misleading markings really matter.

"Get-up"

It will be clear from what we have just said, that cases of passing-off by "get-up" are not very common. Very few manufacturers these days put the real emphasis of their advertising upon the mere look of their package. Even if packages did not change as often as they do, it would still be more sensible to put the real emphasis on a brand name. So the public are taught to look for the name, and they do; and are not deceived by similar packages with a different brand name or none at all. There was a case a few years back (*White, Hudson* v. *Asian*, 1965) where the court held that merely to use an orange-coloured wrapper for wrapping cough-sweets was passing-off; but it happened in Singapore, where many customers could not read the names printed in European lettering on the rival wrappers. The evidence was that the plaintiff's sweets were there known and asked for simply by words meaning "red paper cough sweets." More recently, in *Reckitt & Colman* v. *Borden* 1990, the plaintiffs, who sold lemon juice in a plastic lemon carrying a loose label, were able to prove that the defendant's plastic lemon, although it also carried a loose but different label, would deceive customers. The case was exceptional, however. The plaintiffs were able to prove that the customers not only did not bother to look at the label, but also that they cared about the make of lemon juice (as an American judge with the improbable name of Learned Hand once put the point: "what moves the customers to buy?"). The plaintiffs were also able to prove actual deception by stationing solicitors behind refrigerators in supermarkets on Pancake Day, the solicitors asking people who had picked up the defendants' lemon what they thought they had. Despite some predictions to the effect that this plastic lemon case would spawn many more passing-off actions, it remains the fact that get-up cases are rare precisely because most people do read the labels on most things.

Business names

Many passing-off actions have been concerned with business names, just because these could not be registered as trade marks. (They are now, largely registrable as service marks.) Actions about business names are much like actions about trade marks: the plaintiff has to show on the one hand that people have come to associate the name in dispute with him, on the other that the defendant's version of it is misleadingly similar to his. In judging similarity, it is particularly important what sort of customers are concerned, and this may depend on use of the name in advertising. If the defendant's name is merely used as a company name, in dealings with other companies and so on, it may remain unknown to anyone not capable of telling the two businesses apart. Once it gets advertised to the general public they may be confused by it.

Exceptional cases

In certain special cases, the law accepts as inevitable a certain amount of confusion, and the court will not interfere so long as the defendant does nothing dishonest and nothing to make matters worse.

Use of own name

People have a right to use their own name in business, even though they have a surname that is better known in the trade concerned as the name or mark of someone else. But a man who takes unfair advantage of the possession of such a name will be restrained from doing so; and the books record far more cases where the courts have interfered with the use men were making of their own names than cases where the court has let them go on. In particular, there is no special case of an already established business becoming a company and merely adding "Limited" to its old name. (An established company may claim a right to trade under its name very much as an individual may; but if a new company is formed with a name that is confusingly similar to that of some other business, the court will usually order it to change that name.) Nor is there any special right to trade under one's surname alone; nor any special right to mark one's name on goods, where the general public may see it and be misled by it. Readers needing further warning of the dangers of assuming a right to trade under one's own name may care to look at *Wright's* case 1949 and the *Parker-Knoll* case 1962, or, more recently, the *Gucci* case 1991.

Descriptive names and marks

Those who choose to carry on business under a name which does little more than describe the business cannot complain if others do the same, and must put up with quite small differences between their trading name and other people's. Thus in a case (1946) between rival office-cleaning companies, it was held that the names "Office Cleaning Services" and "Office Cleaning Association" were not too close. In the same way, those who choose as trade marks words which virtually describe the goods should not complain if others describe their goods in similar terms: "Oven Chips" is the sort of thing which the courts will not protect, *McCain* v. *Country Fair*, 1981. But in all these cases, the court will intervene if the defendant is dishonest. A defendant who is trying to get his goods or business mistaken for someone else's will find the court very ready to believe that he has succeeded.

Marks that the public treats as descriptions

Special difficulties arise with those very well-known trade marks that the general public treat as merely the name of the article concerned. If a man goes into an ironmonger's shop and asks for a new Yale lock, he may be wanting one made by the Yale people themselves, but he may just mean that he wants an ordinary pin-tumbler cylinder lock without caring whom it is made by. There may be genuine confusion between him and the shop assistant as to which is meant; or a dishonest shopman may use the ambiguity as an excuse. As one of the *Aertex* cases 1953 illustrates, this may make it very hard for the owner of such a mark to prevent its misuse.

It may be noted that the courts have held that, on the one hand, where a former trade mark had become descriptive adding the word "Genuine" to it did not make it into a trade mark again ("Genuine Staunton" for Staunton-pattern chessmen: *Jacques* v. *"Chess,"* 1940) whilst on the other, use of someone else's trade mark is not made permissible by adding the word "type." A Scottish judge has indeed described the word "genuine" as almost as sinister in significance as the word "type" (*"Harris Tweed,"* 1964).

Geography, the wine and "class" cases

It may be as misleading to say, untruly, that goods come from a particular area (as with "Scotch whisky") as to use the wrong trade mark on them. In such cases, any trader who has a legitimate claim to use the place name concerned for his goods may sue the trader who misuses it for passing-off (*"Spanish Champagne,"* 1960). But place names, and especially anglicised place names, may become merely descriptive of things made in a particular fashion. If so, anyone who genuinely makes his product that way may use the mark, though its use on the wrong sort of goods may still be passing-off (See *"Advocaat"* 1979).

There may be intermediate cases in which the meaning of a geographical term or other description may depend on context. Thus it has been held that "Champagne" necessarily connotes wine (of a particular sort) from the Champagne district of France, and that its use for similar wine made in Spain cannot be justified even if it is expressly labelled "Spanish champagne." So also with "Elderflower Champagne." "Sherry" is to some extent ambiguous: used alone, it connotes wine (of a particular sort) from the Xeres region of Spain, but such expressions as "British sherry" are legitimate (*"Sherry"* 1967). These wine names are getting increased protection under EC regulations: for instance the use of "British Sherry" is shortly to be forbidden.

In all these cases the class of people who genuinely use the mark lose trade to the man who falsely uses the mark. A logical extension of the rule includes cases where the plaintiff uses some official approval mark (*e.g.* a Ministry of Agriculture and Fisheries number) to indicate compliance by his product of certain regulations, and the defendant falsely uses such a mark to indicate he complies too. It seems probably that the courts will support such an action as passing-off, though a case has yet to get to full trial. The nearest the trade mark system has to this sort of thing is the "certification trade mark" (see Chap. 12).

ODD AND UNUSUAL INSTANCES

Where the plaintiff does not trade

There can be passing-off even though there is no trade or business in the ordinary sense concerned; thus the professional institutions can (and now and again, have to) sue both people who put letters after their names so as falsely to pretend to a professional qualification, and people who form societies with similar initials so as to give members something they can put after their names. There have been passing-off actions about *noms-de-plume* as well as about the titles to books and plays. But there has to be some sort of business connection, in a wide sense, between the plaintiff and the sort of thing the defendant is doing, so that the court can be satisfied that there is a real likelihood of the plaintiff's suffering damage to some sort of business interest if the defendant goes on with what he is doing. Thus Mr. Stringfellow, the owner of a famous nightclub, failed to stop a company calling its long thin frozen chips "Stringfellows" because the court thought that he was not really suffering damage (*Stringfellow* v. *McCain* 1984), and the founder of a small political party called the Social Democrats could not stop the use of that title by the latter, more famous, party (*Kean* v. *McGivan* 1982).

In recent years there have been a number of cases concerning merchandising rights in popular characters. They arise in the following way: a manufacturing organisation takes a well-known television or radio personality—real, fictional or even mythical—and exploits the popularity of the character in the advertising and selling of his goods. The question arises: can the character concerned (or in the case of fictional and mythical characters, their creators) take action to prevent such exploitation? Again, the answer turns on whether a reasonable man would think that there was any business connection or "common field of activity" between the plaintiff and the defendant. Thus, it was held that a well-known broadcaster could not sue to prevent the giving to a breakfast food of the name he used on radio (*"Uncle Mac"* 1947), whilst in interlocutory proceedings the court have refused to restrain a builders' skip hire business from using the name of mythical television creatures (*Wombles* v. *Wombles Skips* 1975). In another case (*Taverner Rutledge* v. *Trexapalm*, *"Kojak"* 1975), a lollipop manufacturer, who had taken a franchise to use the name of a television character associated with lollipops, found himself enjoined from using the name (pending a full trial) at the suit of a rival manufacturer who had built up a reputation selling lollipops under the name without taking a licence. More recently the courts have tended to be more favourable to protection of characters. Thus in the case of Teenage Mutant Ninja Turtles (*Mirage Studios* v. *Counter-feat* 1991) a defendant who sold T-shirts with pictures reminiscent (but not enough to infringe copyright) of the turtles was held to be passing-off. The court said that most people expected this sort of thing to be licensed, and so the public would be deceived by "non-genuine" goods. What may have been overlooked is that the public were probably not interested in whether or not there was a licence, what they wanted was what they got, the T-shirt with the design in question.

Authors and artists have special protection from the Copyright, Patents and Designs Act 1988, against attribution to them of works that are not theirs or works of theirs that have been altered (see below).

Other odd instances

The ordinary case of passing-off concerns the sale of goods in such a way that purchasers will be deceived or confused as to whose goods they are. But there can be passing-off where the goods come from the right manufacturer: by selling secondhand goods as new, or spoilt goods as sound, or lower-priced goods as superior ones. There can be passing-off where sellers are confused as to the identity of the buyer instead of the other way round. There can be passing-off where the defendant's name cannot be objected to and it is his address that is confusing. A single case will illustrate these last two possibilities (*Pullman* v. *Pullman* 1919). The defendant, a former director of the family firm, many years later set up on his own, under his own name (as he was entitled to do). Then he altered the name of his house to resemble that of one of the plaintiff's factories (in itself, probably legitimate: it is not passing-off to call a private house by a name confusingly similar to that of someone else, so long as no business is involved). But he then moved his business office to his house and wrote from that address to people who had been supplying the plaintiffs with materials, offering to buy from them. That was held to be passing-off. More recently, in *Bristol Conservatories* v. *Conservatories Custom Built* 1989, the defendants showed photographs of conservatories to potential customers falsely claiming that they, the defendants had built them. In fact the photographs were of the plaintiffs' work. This was also held to be a type of passing-off.

SUING FOR PASSING-OFF

Most ordinary actions for passing-off follow one of two patterns. One is, that the plaintiff at once, on learning of the passing-off. He starts the action and at once applies to the court for an interlocutory injunction to stop the passing-off temporarily, until the case can be brought to trial. It takes about a month for the parties to prepare written evidence from a few important witnesses and bring the case in front of a judge, who decides on the spot whether the case justifies a temporary injunction or not. By that time, both parties know enough of the strength of the other side's case to have quite a good idea of how the trial is likely to turn out, so there is no point in actually fighting the action any further.

The other pattern goes like this. The plaintiff waits for months, or even years, before taking any action. It is of course too late to ask the court for an interlocutory injunction; it is the plaintiff's own fault that the case was not tried long ago. There is no way the parties can accurately assess each other's cases, or see how the matter looks to a judge, without taking the dispute to trial. At the trial, the plaintiffs must prove at length, by evidence from those concerned with the trade, how well known their business or their goods are and how confusing whatever the defendant is doing is. The defendant for his part produces witnesses who have never heard of the plaintiffs; witnesses who by that time have got used to the two parties having similar names or similar trade marks (or whatever the dispute is about); witnesses who are too alert to be confused by any state of affairs worth arguing over at all. The trial will be long and expensive, because of the large number of witnesses. The outcome will be uncertain, because of the difficulty of knowing how the evidence will turn out and what the judge will think of the witnesses. Furthermore, by the time the case comes to trial the trade and public generally have got used to having these two businesses or trade marks about and have learnt to distinguish them; so that what was passing-off when it started may have ceased to cause serious confusion by the time the case comes to trial.

The moral is left to the reader.

14

SLANDER OF GOODS

THE GENERAL RULE

THIS chapter deals with a different sort of unfair competition, known variously as trade libel, slander of goods, slander of title, or malicious or injurious falsehood. It consists of injuring someone else's business, by making, from some "indirect or dishonest motive," a false statement to some third person. To prove dishonest motive is not always easy. Generally the statement must be so false that the defendant cannot have believed it to be true. Real financial loss (or the real risk of it) must be shown by the plaintiff.

The law on this matter is best seen by considering a few examples.

EXAMPLES

De Beers v. *General Electric*, 1975

The plaintiffs and the defendants were both manufacturers of abrasives made from diamonds. The defendants had circulated to prospective customers a pamphlet purporting to show by the results of scientific tests that the plaintiffs' products were inferior to those of the defendants. On an application by the defendants to strike the action out as disclosing no reasonable cause of action, it was held that when "puffing" of goods turns to denigration of the goods of a rival, there comes a point where this becomes actionable, and that if reasonable man might consider than an untrue claim was being made seriously, and with malice, then the plaintiff disclosed a reasonable cause of action.

Greers v. *Pearman & Corder*, 1922

The defendants had a registered trade mark. It included the words "Banquet Brand," but the register included a disclaimer of any exclusive right to the use of those words. The plaintiffs, who were manufacturers in the same trade, used the word "Banquet" as a name for one of their lines. The defendants' solicitor (for whose actions the defendants were responsible) wrote to the plaintiffs' customers claiming that this was an infringement of the registered trade mark, and thereby spoilt the sales of the line concerned. The judge told the jury that if the letters were written in the honest belief that there was an infringement they must give a verdict for the defendants; but if the letters were not written honestly they must find for the plaintiffs. The solicitor, as well as the defendant company's secretary, knew that the entry in the Trade Mark Register included the disclaimer, and the jury found for the plaintiffs.

Hayward & Co. v. Hayward & Sons, 1887

The defendants, having brought a passing-off action against the plaintiffs and lost, issued advertisements that made it look as if they had won. The plaintiffs brought another action, successfully, to get these advertisements stopped.

Mentmore v. Fomento, 1955

The defendants had sued a third party for infringement of patent and had won; but there was an appeal from the decision to the House of Lords still on foot. The plaintiffs were (or so at least the defendants thought) infringing the same patent. The defendants solicitor approached Selfridge's, just at a critical moment from the of view of the Christmas trade, and indicated to the buyer that if the plaintiffs' goods were not withdrawn from sale at once the defendants would get an injunction against the store. What he actually said was "there will be a little court job again." The defendants knew very well that, until the appeal had been decided, they would get no injunction against other infringers. The court granted an injunction to stop the defendants telling people about their successful patent action without disclosing the full facts.

Riding v. Smith, 1876

The false statements concerned need not relate directly to the business. This was a case where the plaintiff's trade decreased, because of rumours that his wife, who served in his shop, had committed adultery. It was held that this was good ground for an action.

Compaq v. Dell, 1992

Dell's advertisement showed pictures of computers in pairs, one of theirs and one of Compaq's. Under each was a price and the accompanying text said that the computers were "basically and essentially the same." The judge held they were not and granted an injunction. Obviously this sort of comparison involves a question of degree (for instance in one pair the Compaq computer had 50 per cent. more memory). Had the difference been less marked the defendants might have succeeded with only a slightly unfair comparison.

CONCLUSION

Enough examples have been given to show the scope of this sort of action. It must not be assumed that such actions would always be won by the plaintiffs; traders are apt to say that other people's goods are worse than theirs, and even where such statements are demonstrably false a judge will not necessarily decide that they are dishonest. There is this further difficulty (*cf.* what was said at the end of the previous chapter, about suing for passing-off) that interlocutory injunctions are very rarely granted in these cases, if the defendant intends to try at the trial to show that what he said was true. The *Compaq* case was an exception: the judge found that no jury could reasonably conclude that the statement was true. A case the other way is *Bestobell* v. *Bigg*, 1975. The defendant decorators had painted a house on the South Circular Road brown. The paint started to turn green with hideous effect. The defendant said the paint was no good but the paint company said he had mixed and applied it wrongly. To make his point the defendant put up a large notice for all to see saying "This house was painted with Carson's paint," clearly implying the paint was indeed no good. An interlocutory injunction was refused because the defendant intended to justify at trial. (Incidently a trade mark injunction was also refused, because the defendant was not trading in paint.)

Litigation is always uncertain, however, and it is wisest not to do anything that can result in an action reaching a court. The safe rule is never to make disparaging statements about a rival business or its products. It should not be forgotten that if such statements hurt anybody's feelings an expensive libel-type action may result—and in these days, the feelings of limited companies are rather easily hurt.

15

THE CRIMINAL LAW

INTRODUCTION

THERE are a variety of Acts of Parliament dealing with methods of trading which are so objectionable as to be made criminal. Most of these Acts are concerned with particular types of goods or trading. For instance there is the Hallmarking Act 1973 and all sorts of provisions in and regulations made under the Food and Drugs Act 1955. Sometimes these regulations are also made under EC directives, *e.g.* the Chocolate Regulations which extend to about 15 pages and are the reason for such odd names as "chocolate flavoured biscuits." It is outside the scope of this book to discuss them. But the Trade Descriptions Act 1968 is of general application.

THE TRADE DESCRIPTIONS ACTS 1968–72

It is a criminal offence to apply a "false trade description" to any goods, or to supply (or offer to supply) any goods to which such a "false trade description" has been applied. The words "trade description" are defined almost as widely as one can possibly imagine. They consist of "an indication, direct or indirect, and by whatever means given, of any of the following matters with respect to any goods or parts of goods, that is to say—(a) quantity, size or gauge; (b) method of manufacture, production, processing or re-conditioning; (c) composition; (d) fitness for purpose, strength, performance, behaviour or accuracy; (e) any [other] physical characteristics; (f) testing by any person and results thereof; (g) approval by any person or conformity with a type approved by any person; (h) place or date of manufacture, production, processing or reconditioning; (i) person by whom manufactured, produced, processed or reconditioned; (j) other history, including previous ownership or use."

A "trade description" can be applied to goods in almost any manner, including orally or in advertisements. No offence is committed unless the "trade description" is false. This ordinarily means that the public must be likely to be misled by the trade description into purchasing the goods. Thus in *Kingston* v. *F. W. Woolworth*, 1968, decided under the old law, the court held that the description "Rolled Gold" applied to a pair of cuff-links sold by the defendants for 4s. was not an offence even though only the fronts of the cuff-links were coated with a thin layer of poor quality gold. On the other hand, if the trade description is completely false, it probably does not matter if the public will be misled or not. Thus in *Kat* v. *Diment*, 1950, the expression "non-brewed vinegar," when applied to something which was not in fact vinegar, constituted an offence even though there was no indication that the public would be misled. Sometimes traders apply a false description and also disclaim liability. Normally this will not work. The Act has recently been brought into play to deal with some publishers who have the misfortune to have a best selling author die. Attempts to put out books by a ghost-author as though they were by the dead author have been punished by magistrates.

The Act has similar provisions dealing with descriptions of services and accommodation. Thus false descriptions of holidays and holiday accommodation have been well kept down by the Act after a number of successful prosecutions. "Right on the beach" would not do for a man-made sandpit—an extreme example which really happened and was really defended. The Act also attempts to deal with unfair price tags (such as "3p off" tags on articles which in fact were never sold for the higher price). And estate agents have recently been brought within the Act.

The practical working of the Acts

(i) As An Alternative to Civil Action

Though the scope of the Act is vast, civil proceedings by a trader affected by their breach are almost always preferable if, as is generally the case, there is also a civil wrong. This is for a number of reasons: firstly the civil court has power to grant an injunction to restrain further acts of the type complained of and, in many cases, an injunction can be obtained very quickly; secondly the award of costs in a civil court is much higher than in a criminal court; thirdly the procedure in a civil court is, generally speaking, much easier than in a criminal court; fourthly the criminal court has no power to award damages or an account of profits; finally the result even of a successful prosecution is unlikely to be more than the imposition of a small fine. Most cases are in the magistrates' court where the maximum fine is £2,000. It is possible for a case to be tried by a higher court before a jury and there a two years' prison sentence could be imposed. In practice a case warranting this would also be a case of fraud of other kinds.

It follows that in practice the Act has had their main application not in the field of protecting traders against unfair competition but rather in the field of the protection of the public at large—"consumer protection." To some extent the two overlap: thus some trading standards officers have recently taken action against blatant pirates, such as market traders selling pirate jeans or counterfeit blank cassettes.

(ii) Enforcement provisions

Unlike earlier Acts upon the same subject, the Trade Descriptions Act makes someone responsible for their enforcement. It is the duty of local trading standards authorities (who employ inspectors) to take proceedings, and they are empowered to make test purchases, enter premises (subject to certain conditions), and seize goods for the purpose of ascertaining whether an offence has been committed. To a certain extent the local inspectors are subject to control by the Board of Trade, which can, for instance, prevent multiple prosecutions.

At the moment action is only taken on simple, plain cases where the public is in need of protection quickly, and it would appear that in most cases inspectors only act if they receive a number of complaints from the public. There is certainly nothing to prevent anyone who feels injured by another's passing-off or infringement of a mark from reporting the matter to a local inspector: this will generally produce some result, if only a warning letter to the culprit.

The Act does not give a trader who suffers particular injury by a breach of their provisions any civil remedy as such, although there may also be a corresponding civil wrong, *e.g.* passing-off.

(iii) Trade marks and the Acts

It might be thought that if the Registrar of Trade Marks were prepared to let a trade mark be registered its use by the owner upon goods within the registration would not be an offence under the criminal law. This is not so. Therefore, whenever a trader is considering a new mark for one of his products or services he should not only choose a mark which is registrable, but also one which will not cause him any trouble with the criminal law. It would be best for him to ensure that in use his mark could not, even remotely, be said to be a "false trade description." (This is yet another reason why totally meaningless words often make the best marks.)

We have already referred to the difficulties which can occur in relation to licensing the use of marks (see Chap. 11). Further difficulties may arise under the Trade Descriptions Act; for example a trade mark used by someone with the permission of the owner may well give "a false indication, direct or indirect ... of the person by whom goods are manufactured or produced."

Finally in relation to trade marks, we should point out that the use of a certification trade mark either by an unauthorised user or otherwise than in accordance with the rules is an offence, for the wide words of the definition of "trade description" (in particular items (g) and (b)) are clearly enough to cover such cases.

CONCLUSION

Although the Act is drafted in such wide terms it are used mainly in flagrant cases: borderline cases and ingenious defendants remain the problems of the civil courts.

PART IV
COPYRIGHT

16

INTRODUCTION TO COPYRIGHT

INTRODUCTION

WE discussed in Chapter 6 the use of copyright law to protect industrial designs; but that is not what the Copyright Acts were meant for. They were meant for the protection of authors, artists and composers and to provide a legal foundation for the innumerable transactions by which authors, artists and composers are paid for their work. This chapter is concerned with the wider field of copyrights.

THE NATURE OF COPYRIGHT

The primary function of copyright law is to protect from exploitation by other people the fruits of a man's work, labour, skill or taste. This protection is given by making it unlawful, as an "infringement of copyright," to reproduce or copy any "literary, dramatic, musical or artistic work" without the consent of the owner of the copyright in that work. It is works that are protected and not ideas; if ideas can be taken without copying a "work," the copyright owner cannot interfere. This distinction is a difficult one to draw, both theoretically and practically; it is discussed in some detail in Chapter 19. Here is an example. If a photograph is taken of a landscape, that photograph will be copyright: good or bad, it counts as an "artistic work." It will be an infringement of copyright (subject to exceptions dealt with in Chap. 20) if, without consent, that photograph is reproduced—either in the sense in which a newspaper would "reproduce" it by making blocks from it and using them for printing, or in the sense in which it could be said to be copied, if an artist were to sit down with the photograph in front of him and make a painting out of it. But it would not be an infringement for another photographer to take a similar photograph of the same landscape: the landscape is not copyright, for the photographer did not make it (the position might be different if he had), and the second photograph, though using the idea of the first, would not be a reproduction of it.

COPYRIGHT, REPUTATIONS AND COMPETITION

Nor is it the function of copyright to protect personal or business reputations, or to prevent business or professional competition: it can sometimes be useful for such purposes, but these uses are in a sense accidental. Thus it is no infringement of copyright to imitate an author's literary style, or to take the title of one of his books, or, probably, even to write a book including characters he has invented —though any of these things may be unlawful for other reasons, *e.g.* if people are misled into thinking that the original author is responsible for the imitation. Thus also it is normally no infringement of copyright to copy another firm's brand name or one of their advertising slogans. (Here again such acts are likely to be unlawful for reasons discussed elsewhere in this book.) It may or may not be an infringement of copyright to use a photograph of a respectable actress to adorn the cover of a disreputable magazine: it depends on who owns the copyright in that photograph, and whether it is a publicity photograph issued for general use. The actress's remedy for that sort of thing is an action for libel or (if the photograph was taken for private or domestic purposes) for infringement of her moral rights (see Chap. 23).

On the other hand, if in such a case the actress does happen to control the copyright in her photograph, an action for infringement of copyright is likely to provide the quickest and cheapest way of dealing with the matter. So also, though an advertising slogan will probably not have a copyright, a complete advertising brochure is likely to be copyright as a "literary work," while any photograph or drawing in it is likely to be copyright as an "artistic work." Such works may be trivial from an artistic or literary point of view, but they have to be very trivial before they lose protection altogether, and commercially they may have great value. A trade mark may consist of a picture— like the "His Master's Voice" dog—or of one of the "house logos" so fashionable nowadays, and the copyright in the picture or logo might be of great value in supplementing ordinary trade mark protection. A fake painting may well be built up largely of bits painted from genuine ones; if it is, and the genuine ones are not so old that their copyright has expired, the fake will infringe and a copyright action may offer the best way of dealing with it.

Types of Copyright Dispute

Copyright disputes (other than disputes about industrial designs) tend consequently to fall into three groups. There are the rare straight-forward cases where a substantial work such as a computer program or video film has been pirated for its own sake. There are also many cases where the original work has little intrinsic value or has not been reproduced in any ordinary sense, and where copyright is invoked for ulterior reasons, usually of a commercial character. In between come those cases where the work copied is a substantial one embodying a great deal of skill or labour—a directory or a time-table or something of that sort perhaps—but nevertheless its value derives more from such things as goodwill than from the labour put into it. In cases in these last two groups there is apt to be a lot of argument as to whether copyright law applies to the case at all.

Copyright in Practice

Although reported copyright disputes tend to fall mainly into these last two groups, the practical and commercial importance of the copyright system lies elsewhere. The main function of the copyright system is to provide a legal foundation for transactions in "rights": to provide a legal sanction behind the customary arrangements by which, for instance, a composer is remunerated when some of his music is used on radio or in a film. It is very rare for such matters to give rise to litigation, and very rare for people outside the particular industry to be concerned with them or to find out much about them.

Copyright and Confidence

It is not the function of copyright to prevent betrayal of confidence, whether personal or commercial. But the conditions under which English law protects confidences as such are somewhat limited (they are discussed in Chap. 22), and copyright may be a valuable additional weapon. For instance, an ordinary business letter may be indiscreet without being confidential, and may fall into the hands of competitors without any illegality that will allow the courts to intervene. But even a business letter is a "literary work" and so copyright. There may be no way to stop a competitor into whose hands it falls from showing it to customers, but he can be stopped from making copies of it for circulation. There is sometimes a close relationship between copyright and confidence. For example, in the *Spycatcher* cases, it was suggested by the House of Lords that the Crown might have copyright in Peter Wright's book (*Att. Gen.* v. *Guardian Newspapers*, 1990).

COPYRIGHT LAW UNTIL THE 1988 ACT

As we have said, copyright was originally intended to protect authors, artists and composers, not industrial designers or engineers. The ancient history of copyright in books is a bit like the modern history of television broadcasting—the Crown assumed a royal prerogative of granting licenses to printers. These licenses were highly profitable for the King and gave him an opportunity to keep printers of seditious material in line. In the sixteenth century, decrees of the Star Chamber were used to keep printers in check. There were common law rights which gave authors (and of course the Crown, which never turned down an opportunity for profit) a limited right to share damages from book pirates.

The first real copyright act, the Statute of Anne 1709, gave authors of books the sole right and liberty of printing them for a term of 14 years. "Books and other writings" was held to include musical compositions, *Bach* v. *Longman*, 1777 and dramatic compositions *Storace* v. *Longman*, 1809. In the former case J. C. Bach sued the publishers for reproducing harpsichord and viol di gamba sonatas. Lord Mansfield said: "A person may use the copy by playing it; but he has no right to rob the author of the profit by multiplying copies and disposing of them to his own use." This is an early instance of a recurring theme in copyright law: if something is worth copying, it is worth protecting. That principle has heavily influenced the courts and Parliament for the last two-hundred years.

There were further Copyright Acts in 1814, 1842, 1911 and 1956, as well as Acts dealing with specific aspects of copyright, such as the Engraving Copyright Act 1734 (the introduction of which was largely influenced by Hogarth), the Sculpture Copyright Act 1814 and the Dramatic Copyright Act 1833. The period and scope of protection was extended with each passing copyright act, since the lobbying power of persons with most to gain from extended copyright protection usually outweighed that of consumers who had most to lose from it. The current period (in the main, life of the author plus 50 years) derives from the Berne Convention—one of the main international treaties on copyright.

The current copyright Act is the Copyright, Designs and Patents Act 1988 which mainly came into force on August 1, 1989. Although the 1988 Act is long and complex, the basic principles of copyright too have remained unchanged for the last two-hundred years.

The previous 1956 Act is still of major importance since a large number of copyright works were created when it was in force. By and large, if a work had copyright under the 1956 Act it will keep it under the 1988 Act.

One of the original aims of the 1988 Act was to simplify copyright law. That was not realised in practice. (It is probably impossible to make a simple statutory code which deals with something as complex as creativity and its commercial exploitation.) It was also intended to serve as the law for the twenty-first century. That too has not proved possible—the 1988 Act has already been amended in two major ways to deal with compulsory licensing of sound recordings for broadcast and to cope with the problems of reverse engineering in computer software. The 1988 Act has to some extent tried to take copyright law back to its roots—for protecting artistically creative people rather than industrial designs. The latter are supposed to be dealt with by design right, although it remains to be seen how well design right will cope or how much difference this will make in practice.

Old Copyrights

As will be seen in Chapter 17, copyright lasts a very long time. There are still many works in existence that have copyright although they were created before the present Act (or even its predecessor) came into force, and to some extent it is necessary in dealing with them to refer to the old law. For most purposes, the position is, that if such works are copyright at all, they are governed by the present law; they may, however, have lost copyright (or never have had it) although by present-day reckoning they are still new enough to have a copyright still in force. Such cases are not of sufficient practical importance to justify detailed discussion of the old law in a book such as the present one. It is usually sufficient to remember that if a work had copyright before August 1, 1989, its copyright continues after that date.

"REPRODUCTION"

It has already been pointed out that the word "reproduce" as used in copyright law has rather different meanings in different contexts. This difficulty runs right through our copyright law. If we speak of one book being copied from another, this is not the same sort of "copying" as occurs when (for example) a painting is made into a plate to illustrate a book. In fact the "copyright" in a work of literature and the "copyright" in a painting are not really quite the same sort of thing: the "copyright" in a song is again something rather different. Nor is the legal protection needed by the author, or by the publisher of a novel, really the same as that needed by the author of a song (who is mainly concerned to stop its being sung or recorded without payment) or by an architect (who is mainly concerned to ensure that anyone wanting a house such as he would design will employ him as architect rather than a competitor). A sculptor on the other hand will get his main protection from the general law of property, and her copyright is unlikely to be of great value. The Act does differentiate between different categories of "works," as we shall see, but for many purposes it lumps them all together.

The word "reproduction" is, however, not used in copyright law in the sense in which music is often said to be "reproduced" by a wireless or a record player. That, in copyright language is "performance by means of a mechanical instrument" and not "reproduction," and different rules apply to it. The Copyright Act in fact speaks of reproduction "in a material form": it is the record itself (or the printed score) that is the "reproduction."

WORKS THE SUBJECT OF COPYRIGHT

"Works"

COPYRIGHT extends to almost everything, published or unpublished, that can be called "a work" at all. The Copyright Act counts among the subjects of copyright: novels and other "literary works"; tables, compilations and computer programs, which count as "literary works"; lectures, addresses, speeches and sermons; plays, scripts for cinema films, dance and mime all of which count as "dramatic works" (the film itself is a work, but of a different category); paintings, drawings, engravings, photographs and similar things (such as photo-lithographs), sculpture, works of "artistic craftsmanship" not covered by any other head, and works of architecture—all counting as "artistic works"; music; gramophone records, tapes, perforated rolls and other devices for reproducing sounds; sound and television broadcasts and cable programmes; and the typography of books. It is of some importance to which category a work belongs since—see Chapter 20—the rights of the copyright owner depend on it. A detailed list of "works" in which copyright can exist is contained in the Note to Chapter 19.

Foreign "works"

Foreign works are protected if they come from a country (or a citizen or resident of a country) with which the United Kingdom has made a treaty to that effect. The foreign countries concerned likewise protect British works more or less as they protect local ones. But some countries (the U.S.A. in particular) used to require copies of the work to be marked © with the name of the copyright owner and the year of first publication.

Merit, originality, and various sorts of works

In general, works are protected regardless of merit. Thus a rather ordinary tie-on business label has been given protection as an "artistic work" (*Walker* v. *British Picker*, 1961), as have drawings of simple machine parts (*British Northrop* v. *Texteam*, 1974). They must be "original," in the sense of not being entirely copies of another similar work—in other words they must "originate" from their authors. So, for example, one would not get a new copyright in a tracing of an old drawing (*Interlego* v. *Tyco*, 1989). They must also be substantial enough to deserve the name of "works," though here again (as the case just mentioned shows) the standard is not high. A ballet need not be good, but must be reduced to writing. But a play is not deprived of copyright because it is a bad play, or a painting because the artist is completely lacking in skill or taste.

Artistic craftsmanship

The term "work of artistic craftsmanship" is not quite clear. In the leading case on the subject (*Hensher* v. *Restawile*, 1975) the members of the House of Lords expressed differing views on its interpretation, but were unanimous in holding that ephemeral, nailed-up prototypes of a three-piece suite were not works of artistic craftsmanship. The expression would include hand-decorated pottery, but a court has hesitated to say that it includes a dress. There has to be something "artistic" as well as an element of "craftsmanship." This can be important when it comes to industrial designs. When a machine part is made from drawings, there will be copyright in the drawing; but when it is made by a craftsman simply playing with a bit of metal until he gets it right, there is no copyright. Unregistered design right has a role to play in protecting works of pure craftsmanship but not *artistic* craftsmanship.

Photographs and sound-recordings

Photographs and sound-recordings are not restricted as to merit or subject matter, but like any other works they cannot be copyright unless they are "original," and this needs some consideration. In a sense, no photograph or sound-recording is original: for the camera or microphone only records what is presented to it. But there is more to making a photograph and much more to making a sound-recording than that, and the skill of the photographer or recording engineer will found copyright just as will the skill of the artist who makes an engraving from a painting. It is the change of form of the work and the skill involved that in these cases justifies copyright. Where there is no change of form, copyright must be justified in some other way; a mere re-photographing of a photographic print, for instance, would not give the second photograph a copyright of its own. For this there would have to be sufficient alteration combined with the re-photographing to make the second a different "work." But it may be assumed that, in any practical case, whoever did the re-photographing could show that enough additional skill and original-ity was put into it to give the new photograph a new copyright. So in the field of sound-recording, whilst a "mere" re-recording would give no additional copyright, in practical cases, such as transfer of a "historic" recording from old 78s on to modern disc or tape, the re-cording company may have done enough work improving the re-cording quality to make it effectively a new recording and so give it a new copyright. This is much the same problem as that of a new edi-tion of a book: see below.

Triviality

In copyright disputes of a commercial character, the main issue in the case is sometimes whether that which has been copied embodies enough "work, labour, skill or taste" to be called an original work. It is not easy to lay down any clear rules as to this, for it is essentially a matter of opinion—of the opinion, that is to say, of whatever court tries the dispute. The opinions of judges are never very easy to fore-cast, for they necessarily depend a great deal on the precise circum-stances of the case in which the issue concerned arises. For instance, few judges can avoid giving some weight to their opinion of the relat-ive merits and morals of the parties to the dispute. Nevertheless, it is possible to give some idea of the probability that a particular "work" will be held to have copyright.

Different authors

The first question that arises, is how much of the "work" derives from any particular author: for it is only the part for which he is res-ponsible that can be considered in deciding whether he has produced an original work. Suppose for instance that a textbook has run, as legal textbooks often do, into a large number of editions in the course of a great many years. The first edition was no doubt copyright; per-haps it still is, perhaps that copyright has lapsed. Each subsequent edition may or may not give rise to a new copyright in the whole book, depending on whether the amount of work done by the editor in producing the new edition is sufficient to be called the creation of a new work. (It does not matter for this purpose whether the new edi-tion is edited by the original author or by someone else; the test is the same in either case.) A similar problem arises in connection with a publication such as a railway time-table, which is reprinted perhaps monthly with very few alterations from one month to the next. In connection with a textbook this question is usually not very hard to answer, though the answer is hard to put into words; one can "feel" the difference between making minor or routine alterations in the book and making a more substantial contribution to the book as a whole. In other cases the distinction may be very hard to draw, and when this is the case courts tend to reach illogical decisions that confuse matters still further. It has, for instance, been held that each successive monthly edition of the Index to a railway time-table had a copyright of its own, although this Index was merely a list of railway-station names, and there were, on the average, only about ten changes made in this list each month. Probably the true moral to be drawn from this particular case, is that if a "work" in fact embodies a great deal of labour, it is unsafe to copy it in reliance upon a purely technical defence to copyright proceedings. For such an Index would clearly have been copyright if it had been produced entirely afresh; the only difficulty arose from its having grown up gradually over a period of many years. It would be a surprising thing, if a work were to be refused copyright merely because it had taken years to produce, and no court would hold this to be the law if it could help it; it is however the law in some cases. On the other side of the line, retracing the drawings for "lego" bricks (adding a few manufacturing directions) has been held not to give rise to a new copyright (*Interlego* v. *Tyco*, 1989).

"*Anything worth copying is worth protecting*"

One way of approaching the problem of where to draw the line between that which amounts to a "work" and that which does not, is to say that anything worth copying is worthy of protection against copying. In many cases this rule is a useful guide. But the line must still be drawn somewhere, and the difficulty of drawing it tends to be most acute just in the sort of case where this rule is not applicable, in those commercial cases where something has been copied, not so much to avoid the trouble of producing something similar, as for extraneous reasons. The most that can be said with certainty is that any sort of drawing may be held to have copyright; that even a few bars of music may have copyright; at any rate if they are recognisable; and that although a single sentence (such as an advertising slogan) has never yet been held to be copyright, anything more may constitute a "literary work." (The title of a book, for example, is not copyright, and protection for it (if any) must be sought in an action for passing-off (see *Exxon*, 1982).) Merit is not necessary, but a composition that is striking—"original" in the ordinary as distinct from the copyright sense—is more likely to be protected by the courts than a common-place composition of the same size or length. Even so, short business letters have been held copyright notwithstanding a characteristic absence of signs of literary skill. So have advertisements in newspapers.

Compilations

It is particularly difficult to lay down rules for determining whether there is copyright in a compilation or arrangement of facts or of non-copyright material. There will clearly be copyright in such things as telephone directories, *Who's Who*, railway time-tables or mathematical tables, if they are "original" in the copyright sense. Messages sent out by news agencies have been held copyright, even where literary form was not involved—as with stock-exchange prices; so have a week's radio programmes; so have the starting prices for a race (which took some skill in sorting out), but not a list of starting positions (which were merely written down as they were determined by ballot); so has an anthology of poems, not themselves copyright; but not an edition of a non-copyright book shortened by cutting out about half of it. (In the last case, there were critical notes published with the new edition and these were held copyright.) Copyright has been refused to a local time-table, made by selecting and rearranging entries from a larger time-table relating to a particular town, and it has been refused to a selection of seven non-copyright tables of conventional type for inclusion in a diary. About all that can be said in general is that mere industry counts less than knowledge, skill or taste in such matters; that the amount of labour that goes into a particular compilation is of great importance; and that anything published in permanent form—a book, for instance—has a better chance of protection than such ephemeral productions as a notice on a notice board. The rest is a matter of how the court feels about it. In the case of the diary, for instance, the Court of Appeal decided one way, the judge who tried the case at the first instance and the House of Lords the other; a sure sign of the sort of case where anything can happen.

An ordinary book of non-fiction may well be copyright on two separate grounds: both from the literary skill that went into writing it and from the skill and labour that went into selecting the facts set out in it. Historical facts for example are not copyright in themselves, but a selection of them can have copyright as a compilation. Here again the line is difficult to draw: a compilation of facts will have copyright, but mere ideas will not.

COPYRIGHT CAN EXIST ONLY IN "WORKS"

It is worth emphasising that apart from questions of amount—of whether there is enough of a product for it to count as a "work" for copyright purposes—nothing can attract copyright unless it is the sort of thing that is called a "work." For instance, it will be an infringement of copyright to film a play without consent, but not to film a dog-show or a boxing match: the one is a "dramatic work," the others are not, for nobody has composed or arranged precisely what happens at them. If the promoters of such spectacles want to prevent photography, they must do it in some such way as by not selling tickets to people who do not agree to not take photographs. So also, a card-index system is not copyright: nor is a game, though the written out rules of the game will be and so may any board on which it is played. Thus the inventor of a new game may be able to prevent other people copying his board or his book of rules. A collection of five-letter code-words was held copyright as a "literary work" (skill was needed in selecting the words so as to guard against errors in transmission) but not a system for coding the wholesale prices in a catalogue: however ingenious a system, and however successful in concealing the retail profit from customers, it was a mere scheme and not a "work." The instructions for decoding the prices could have been copyright: but that copyright would not be infringed by a competitor who wrote his own instructions, quite independently.

ILLEGAL AND IMMORAL WORKS

By way of exception from the general rules, the courts will not protect a work that is illegal, immoral, indecent or similarly undeserving of protection. A libellous poem for instance cannot claim copyright, nor can an obscene picture. Inevitably, a great deal depends on the attitude of the judge trying the case. Late in 1939 for example, copyright protection was refused to a would-be humorous document entitled "The Last Will and Testament of Adolf Hitler"; while not obscene, it was in the view of the judge vulgar and indecent. Presumably however some people thought it funny, or it would not have been worth publishing, let alone worth copying too. The judge concerned was not one of them but, if he had been, the case would probably have gone the other way. Cases of this sort being rare, the limits of this exception have never been very clearly laid down. Recently a doll which revealed what lay beneath the sporran was held entitled to registered design protection. (*Masterman's Design*, 1991).

OVERLAPPING COPYRIGHTS

It is in general irrelevant to the question whether a work is copyright, to consider whether it is covered by some other copyright too. In the case for instance of what are called "collective works"—symposia, magazines, encyclopedias and so on—there must necessarily be a whole series of copyrights in the separate articles or stories as well as a copyright in the work as a whole: in the general plan and arrangement of the work.

Overlapping copyrights are found not only in collective works, however. In Chapter 16, it was pointed out that a painting can be a re-production of a photograph for copyright purposes. In such a case there will be a copyright in the painting separate from that in the original photograph: the painting is an "artistic work" in its own right, requiring skill and labour for its execution, notwithstanding that the scene depicted is taken from a photograph. In such a case it will be unlawful to reproduce the painting unless the owners of both copyrights consent. Similar cases are common in other arts too: for instance, in a record of music, both the music itself and the recording will be copyright, unless the music is quite old. The point is important in dealing in copyright, for it will be ambiguous to refer to "the copyright in the painting," if more than one copyright exists in the painting, and an agreement using such language may have rather unexpected effects. See Chapter 21.

Translations

A translation will have copyright, independently of the work from which it is translated. The classic example of this was a case where the court had to decide upon the ownership of the copyright, if any, in a book said to have been dictated to a "medium" by the spirit of a biblical character who had died some 2,000 years before. The court noted that the book was written, not in any language current in those days, but in somewhat archaic English, and decided that the translation from one language to the other must have been done by the medium—who consequently had a translator's copyright. The case is *Cummins* v. *Bond*, 1926: the full report (1927 1 Ch. 167) is well worth reading as itself a "literary work." It must not be supposed that the judge necessarily believed the book to have been dictated by any spirit; but a judge has to decide an ordinary civil case on such evidence as the parties choose to put it before him. Since both parties accepted that the book had a ghostly origin, it was proper for the judge to decide the case on that basis.

It should be noted that the matter translated need not be anything that is capable of sustaining a copyright; the test to be applied is whether the translator has expended a substantial amount of labour, skill and knowledge upon making his translation. If he has, it will be copyright.

Other cases

In the same way, a shorthand report of a speech has its own copyright; here it is the shorthand-writer's skill and labour from which the copyright derives. The speech will in itself probably be copyright too. The photograph of a painting, or painting made from a photograph; the film made from a book or play and the "book of the film"—are all similar instances. In these cases there are two copyrights (at least): one, that in the original work, covers both works; the other covers the transformed work only. So again an architect's plans will be copyright as plans—unless of course they are merely copied from other plans. If a building is built from the plans it will attract architectural copyright which is quite distinct from the copyright in the plans. Finally, there is a copyright in the typographical arrangement of a published edition of a work, which is separate from the copyright in the work itself: see the Note to Chapter 19.

The Period of Copyright

Copyright in ordinary literary, artistic, musical and dramatic works lasts a very long time: during the author's life and for 50 years after (or rather, until the end of the fiftieth year after that in which the author dies—this rounding-off to the end of the year applies to all periods of copyright). Note, however, that the copyright in artistic works used in industrial designs is the subject of special rules, depending on their date of creation. Literary, musical and dramatic works and engravings will have even longer copyright if they are not exploited (published or performed in public or recorded and sold as records) whilst the author is still alive: in that case the 50-year period begins at the end of the year of first exploitation. For photographs, recordings, films and other more special types of work there are shorter periods, listed in the Note to Chapter 19. Exceptionally, works belonging to the Crown have only a 50-year period (but, as before, it mostly begins with the year of first exploitation). If a work which has Crown Copyright is unpublished, copyright lasts 125 years, from when the work was made. There are similar provisions for works that are genuinely anonymous or pseudonymous—in the sense that the author's identity never really becomes known. If a work has joint authors, the period is taken from the life of whichever dies last. (A work consisting say, of words and music by different people is not a joint work in this sense: the copyright in the words and that in the music may consequently expire at different times.) Most books nowadays carry the year of first publication, and gramophone records now have to; but in general it is not easy to find out when copyright expires.

18

THE OWNERSHIP OF COPYRIGHT

INTRODUCTION

IN considering ownership, it should be remembered that in this country, copyright comes into existence automatically (if at all), without need for formalities. The result is that it is possible for the question of ownership never to arise at all, until the copyright is the subject of some dispute. It will then be necessary to work out who is the owner, with no assistance from registers or formal documents. The rules of law governing ownership are therefore important: fortunately, they are simple too.

This chapter deals with the question of who owns a copyright in the first place; what may happen to it afterwards is a different question altogether and will be considered in Chapter 21.

THE BASIC RULE—COPYRIGHT BELONGS TO THE AUTHOR

Apart from in the situations mentioned below, copyright belongs in the first place to the author of the work concerned. The author, for this purpose, is the person who actually expends the work, labour, knowledge, skill or taste by virtue of which the work is copyright. In the case of a book for instance, the "author" of the letterpress will be whoever composes the sentences of which it is made up. If a person dictates a book to a secretary, she will be the author—not her secretary; if on the other hand she merely provides the ideas, and the secretary writes the book, the secretary is the author—whether the book is published in her name or not. (But see exception (i) below.) If a book is illustrated by drawings, the "author" of the drawings will be whoever drew them, notwithstanding that the idea for each illustration was taken from the book itself. There may of course be books where, although one person wrote the whole text, another provided and selected the material for the book and determined its arrangement to a sufficient extent to be considered a joint author of it. In general however the person who chooses the actual words used will be the sole author: for instance, where a "ghost" writer composes a person's autobiography, the "ghost" will be held to be the sole author even though the subject of the autobiography supplies such facts as may be included. It has even been held that the compiler of a work such as *Who's Who* is the "author" of each of the entries, although the material for the entry is supplied by the person concerned in response to a questionnaire.

In the case of a photograph, the "author", for the purpose of copyright, used to be the person who owns the film at the time when the photograph is taken. Now it is the person who creates it who will be the first owner of any copyright (subject to what is said below).

Exception (i)—Works by employees

When the author of a work is in the employment of some other person "under a contract of service or apprenticeship," and the work is made "in the course of his employment," the copyright belongs to the employer. This does not include cases where the author can be loosely said to be "employed to produce the work," but is not employed in the ordinary sense. Thus the editor or publisher who commissions a book or article gets the copyright only if the author's contract says so; the publisher who employs an author (by a "contract of service") gets the copyright automatically, just as if the man were hired to make boots—there would be no need for a contract saying that the boots would belong to the owner of the factory. In the same way, the architect who is "employed" to design a house does not lose the copyright in his design to the building owner; but the architect's draughtsman, who works for a salary, will be an employee, and the copyright in the plans he is paid to draw will belong to the architect who employs him. The exact limits of the phrase "in the course of his employment" are not very easy to define: it is said that this phrase has given rise to more litigation than any other in the English language. For most purposes however it means simply: that it was part of his job to produce that work. One example is the architectural draughtsman already mentioned. On the other side of the line, there was a case where a translation had been made by a man for his employers, but in his spare time and for extra payment (as distinct from an overtime payment). It was held that the translator, not his employer, was the first owner of the copyright in the translation. (It may be that the employer could have demanded that the copyright be handed over to him; but this question did not arise, for it was not his employer that the translator was suing.) It is not quite clear to whom works of a secretly moonlighting employee belong.

Exception (ii)—"Commissioned works"

There *used to be* an important exception to the general rule that the author was the first owner of copyright (it has now been abolished). This related to commissioned works of certain kinds. If someone commissioned the taking of a photograph or an engraving or painting a portrait, and paid or agreed to pay for it, the commissioner would get copyright automatically in the work made in pursuance of the commission. There were quite a few cases about this—several turning on whether there was payment or an obligation to pay, since, if the sitting was free, the photographer or engraver or portraitist would own the copyright. But although it has been abolished, the exception still applies to works made before the Copyright Designs and Patents Act 1988 came into force. For example, one rather recent case concerned the photographs for use on the Beatles' Sgt. Pepper's Lonely Heart's Club Band album. These photographs were taken in 1967 by Michael Cooper, a fashionable sixties photographer. He and his assistant had taken several rolls of film of the Beatles on the famous set and of them wandering about the studio. The photographs included the one actually used for the cover and several other similar ones— "outtakes." Michael Cooper's son, Adam, wanted to exploit some of these outtakes. The Beatles wanted to stop this and one of the questions raised was who owned the copyright in them? This depended on whether they had been taken pursuant to a commission from the Beatles (or people acting for them) and whether they had paid or agreed to pay for them. The judge held that there was not enough evidence to show that there was a commission prior to the taking of the photographs or that the person doing the commissioning had paid or agreed to pay for them. So the Beatles lost.

There are many situations in which a person commissions another person to do some creative work. Although now the copyright belongs to the creator of the work, this can sometimes cause problems. For example, an engineering company asks an advertising consultant to design a campaign poster. Nothing is said about copyright. Who owns it? Or a managing director of a company does a drawing in her work hours and for company purposes. (She is not an employee but a director, so the first of the employees' exceptions does not apply.) Who owns the copyright in the drawing?

In strict law, in the first case, it will be the advertising consultant and in the second, it will be the managing director. But the courts are not especially comfortable with solutions like that since they can lead to results which no-one really intended at the time. So they occasionally fudge the issue a bit. Some judges take the view that if commercial people and organisations do not make proper provision to regulate their affairs, that is tough: the courts won't spring to their aid. But others will say one of two things: either the engineering company has an implied licence to use the poster design for its campaign or, more rarely, that the company is the "equitable owner" of the copyright. The same will apply in the second example—the company may be held to have an equitable right to the copyright. Being the equitable owner means that you have a right to have the legal title to the copyright transferred into your name. This solution is a way of getting round the problem that the Copyright Act principally gives rights to the creators of the work, but this can sometimes result in the creators holding the people for whom they do the work to ransom.

CROWN COPYRIGHT

Where a work is either made by Her Majesty or by an officer or servant of the Crown in the course of his duties, the copyright belongs to the Crown. There is a separate Parliamentary copyright. The Crown does not always enforce its copyrights and allows such things as Acts of Parliament to be freely reproduced from the official editions published by the Stationery Office; but the copyright is there, and it is enforced in relation even to such apparently public works as Ordnance Survey maps, or directions from Ministries to local authorities. As was stated in the last chapter, copyright in these cases lasts for 50 years from commercial publication; a provision which has the merit that it is possible to find out whether the copyright in Crown works has expired without having first to find out who the author was: an almost impossible task in the case of, say, an Ordnance Survey map.

WHERE AUTHORSHIP IS NOT CERTAIN

If a work appears to be signed, or to bear an author's name, the courts will assume unless it is proved otherwise that the person whose name or signature the work bears is the owner of the copyright in it; if not, the first publisher will be presumed to own the copyright. These are however merely rules of evidence; they do not alter rights, but sometimes make it easier for the plaintiff in a copyright action to prove his case. In particular, they make it possible to sue for infringement of the copyright in an anonymous work without disclosing the author's name.

19

WHAT IS INFRINGEMENT?

INTRODUCTION

IT was pointed out in Chapter 16 that copyright is in essence merely a right to stop other people doing certain things (the "acts restricted by the copyright"). The definition of infringement is consequently of very great importance. The present chapter sets out to explain, just what are these activities that an owner of a copyright is entitled to stop; the rules stated in this chapter are however subject to certain exceptions discussed in the chapter following.

INFRINGEMENT BY REPRODUCTION

First of all, copyright in a work will be infringed if the work is copied without the consent of the owner of the copyright. To give a simple example, consider an article in a magazine. In the ordinary way of course, it will have been sent in by the author (or by her literary agent); sending it in will mean that she owns the copyright and she wants it published so long as she gets the proper fee—and the only possibility of argument lies in the size of the fee. It is only when something goes wrong that a dispute about copyright can arise. Suppose she sends in illustrations with her manuscript and they are not hers to offer for publication; then each copy of the magazine "reproduces" them without the consent of the copyright owner, and that is infringement. (The person who sent the article in pays the damages, if she has the money.) Or the whole article may be very like one that appeared earlier in some other magazine, but not quite the same. This may or may not constitute an infringement of the copyright in the earlier story according to circumstances; and it is necessary to consider in some detail, just where the line is to be drawn.

144

Copying

The Copyright Designs & Patents Act 1988 uses the word "copy" in this connection. This principally involves reproducing the work concerned, or a substantial part of it, in a material form. Copying is essential to this sort of infringement. It has been said often enough that six monkeys, operating typewriters at random, would sooner or later reproduce all the books in the British Museum Library; among them, works that were copyright. But there would be no infringement of the copyright, for there would be no copying: the work would have been reproduced quite accidentally, without reference to the original. So we suggest, as a couple of exercises for the reader, two problems. First, would a novel thus created by the monkeys be copyright, and if so, who would own the copyright? Secondly, if someone goes through the output of the monkeys—or of a computer printing at random—until he finds the complete text of a popular novel (as he must, sooner or later), is publishing that an infringement?

Copying need not be direct, and it need not be conscious or deliberate. All that is necessary for an infringement (so long as a substantial part of the earlier work is taken), is that the later work should somehow, through some channels, be derived from the earlier. On the other hand, this amount of copying is necessary, and must be proved: for if the copyright owner wishes to stop an infringement, she must prove to the appropriate court that infringement has taken place.

Proof of copying

The difficulty of proof is often a serious one. It will very seldom be possible to prove directly that copying has taken place: for only the alleged infringer knows how the work came into existence. The result is that in practice the only thing to do is to point to the resemblances between the two works and to say that these resemblances are too many and too close to be due to coincidence; the court can then be asked to infer that some sort of copying must have taken place. If the court accepts this argument it will then be up to the alleged infringer to explain the resemblances away if possible. That is to say, a reasonable explanation of how those resemblances could have come into existence without any copying must be produced. Not every explanation will do, for judges are not exactly credulous people; if the explanation is that X thought the whole thing up without ever having seen or heard of the earlier work, the judge will want to see X (or hear

some good reason why he cannot see X) and find out whether to believe the story or not. But if the explanation is reasonable, the copyright owner must find some other way of proving the case, and as we
have said, there is usually no other way available. An interesting case
on this point is *Francis Day & Hunter* v. *Bron*, 1963 where the court
held that although there were very great similarities between the
plaintiffs' tune "In a Little Spanish Town" and the defendants' "pop"
song, "Why." This was not enough to prove infringement where the
composer of "Why" (whose story was believed) said he could not remember ever hearing the plaintiffs' tune although he was prepared to
admit that he might have heard it on the radio when he was young.

A substantial part must be copied

When it has been shown that copying has taken place, the next requirement for proving infringement is to show that the part of the
one work reproduced in the other is a substantial part. The question:
what is a substantial part of a work? is very similar to one discussed in
Chapter 17: what is substantial enough to be called a work?

(a) Where a part is copied exactly

Here the principle that what is worth copying is worth protecting
can be given full scope. Once a court is satisfied that there is a copyright work, and that the defendant in the case before it has thought it
worth while copying out word for word some part of that work, it
will be very hard to persuade that court that the part copied was not
substantial. Thus where four lines of a short poem of Kipling were reproduced in an advertisement, the court found no difficulty in holding that this was a substantial enough part of the poem for there to be
infringement. As usual however a lot depends on how the courts feels
about the case. Where for instance the title of a short story was taken
from the refrain of a popular song, and four lines from the song were
printed below the title (as of course quotations often are), the court
held that this was not an infringement of the copyright in the song.
The line must be drawn somewhere: the owner of the copyright in the
song was not really deprived of his property or of an opportunity to
draw profits from his property; and regarded as a literary work, the
song was not quite in the same class as a poem of Kipling.

This question of merit is rather a difficult one. Strictly speaking, it
is not easy to see how the merit of a work should affect the matter at
all. In practice, it is always easier to found a successful action for infringement of copyright upon a work that has merit than upon a
work that has not. The law is never absolutely rigid, and the court will

give a common sense decision where it can. It is fortunate that this is so; but it is sometimes in consequence a little difficult to forecast what a court's decision will be in any particular case. The imponderable influence of merit (or the lack of it) in copyright actions is one of the things that make prediction difficult.

A very instructive case as to what is a substantial part of a work arose from the inclusion, in a newsreel of a military parade, of a sequence taken while the band was playing the copyright march "Colonel Bogey." The sequence lasted less than a minute, and other things were happening at the same time, but the principal air of the march was clearly recognisable. This was held to amount to taking a substantial part of the march; the more so, because the sound-track of the film could have been used by itself as a record of the march—to provide incidental music during an interval for instance. There is now a special provision excluding infringement in cases where music is merely picked up by the microphone of a newsreel camera, and not specially recorded to provide a background to the film.

(b) Compilations

The simplest examples of compilations are of course works like directories, consisting of a large number of short entries without any particular literary form. Here the rule as to infringement is clear. It is a "reproduction," and so an infringement, to take the entries from one directory for use in another, even if they are independently checked against some other source of material and then completely rearranged in combination with other material. It is legitimate, however, after compiling a directory from other sources, to check it against a rival work to see that there are no mistakes or omissions. It is not so clear to what extent entries that are found to have been omitted from the new compilation may at this stage be copied into it from the old: a few may be, a substantial number may not, but exactly how many may be depends upon the circumstances of the case. In particular, it depends a great deal on whether the judge who tries the case really believes that the second work was independently compiled before the checking took place. Compare *Peacey* v. *De Vries*, 1921, where the court believed it, with *Blacklock* v. *Pearson*, 1915, where the court obviously did not.

The same rule as for directories has been applied to a translation of a foreign play, and is probably applicable to any work considered as a collection of information. That is to say, where a work has copyright by reason of the skill and labour that went to collecting the information given in it, that copyright will not be infringed by using the work as one source among others, to supplement and correct information obtained in the main elsewhere. The copyright will, however, be infringed, if any substantial part of the information set out by the work is taken as a whole, even if it is afterwards cross-checked against other sources. This is, of course, not the only test of infringement: for most works will also have copyright by reason of their literary or artistic form, and this latter copyright will be infringed if the form is taken whether the information set out is taken or not. To this question of reproduction of form we must now turn.

(c) Where there is merely a similarity of form

In discussing this question, it must first of all be remembered that there is no copyright in ideas. Thus an illustrated joke, for instance, will have copyright as a picture, and possibly even the words of the caption might be copyright: but the joke itself cannot be. There will consequently be no infringement if the same joke is used by someone else, differently phrased and with a different picture. In the same way it is no infringement of copyright to take the plot of a book, even in fair detail. In one case, for instance, there was issued with a set of gramophone records of operatic music a fairly full synopsis of the action of the opera: this was held not to be an infringement of the libretto of the opera. Nor would the position be in any way different if that synopsis had been written up into a complete new libretto for a similar opera: for there would have been nothing common to the two works except the synopsis, and this did not infringe any copyright.

It must also be remembered that every competent worker in any field must be expected to be familiar with any important work that has gone before; and it is just the important and successful work, that everyone ought to know and that will inevitably influence works that come after it, that is likely to attract infringers. In fiction it is indeed often the poor and unknown author whose unexpectedly brilliant work is stolen, but in real life that sort of thing seems not to be a commercial proposition. The inevitable influence of one work on those that follow it does not involve infringement of copyright. The difficulty is to distinguish between drawing on the common stock of experience, and making improper use of other people's work.

Judges have tried to express the way the line is to be drawn, by saying that for there to be infringement, one work must produce the "same effect" as the other. To put it slightly differently, there must be something that might make people encountering the two works in succession feel, "I have read this story—or seen this play—or heard this music—before." Some examples may help to explain how such tests work out in practice.

Example 1:

Many years ago, one Austin composed a new arrangement of the music of a work that had long ago lost any copyright it had ever possessed: the "Beggar's Opera." The new arrangement was of course copyright; it was also a popular success. A manufacturer of gramophone records, wishing to take advantage of Austin's success, brought out a recording of extracts from the "Beggar's Opera." Since the tunes were all old, this was not in itself any infringement of Austin's copyright. But the recording went further: although the actual notes were not copied from the Austin arrangement, the tunes were "dressed up in the same way," as the judge put it. That was infringement: a record is a "reproduction." The case in fact raised in a different context the same question as the example discussed in Chapter 16, of the photographer who sees a successful photograph of a landscape and goes and takes another like it. He may photograph the same view, for there is no more copyright in a view than there was in the tunes of the "Beggar's Opera." But he must not go further and imitate to any substantial extent the tricks by which the first photographer has converted the view into a successful photograph.

The Austin case illustrates also the way in which the circumstances of a case influence the court's findings. The defendants there had advertised their records in a way that emphasised the relation with Austin's successful arrangement, and in fact in this connection lay the whole reason for bringing out those records at that time at all. This made it by no means easy for the defendants to argue that they had really taken nothing from Austin: the defence was in effect merely that, as a technical legal matter, what they had done was not reproduction of a substantial part of that which was the subject of copyright. Purely technical defences are always dangerous. If such a question arises on a comparison of two apparently independent works, the case is not prejudiced by any admissions that the one work is connected with the other, and such a defence takes on a rather different aspect. The defendant can, and does, argue that there has been no copying at all in any ordinary sense; that the resemblances between the two works if not pure coincidence—any two works being indeed much more alike than perhaps their authors would admit—are the result of the sort of unconscious influence mentioned above as inevitable and legitimate; and that these resemblances are trivial, not substantial. (He may even argue that the resemblances are due to legitimate "quotation" of phrases that the hearer will be expected to recognise as coming from earlier works.) Only then does he argue that in any case, what is common to the two works is not the sort of thing that the law calls "reproduction." If there is real doubt as to the copying, the technical defence will have a much more favourable reception.

Example 2:

Bauman was a photographer of high repute who took pictures for the "Picture Post" magazine. One of them was of two fighting cocks which he took in Cuba. Fussell was a painter. He saw Bauman's photograph in the Picture Post, cut it out, pinned it to his studio wall and from it painted a picture of two fighting cocks in the same position and attitude as the birds in the photograph. In the painting, the colouring was different as was the general effect of the painting, which was not at all photographic. Experts were lined up on each side, including the Arts Director of the Arts Council and Professor Moyniham, a well known painter from the Royal College of Art. The Court of Appeal judges (who were divided 2:1) spoke of the "feeling and artistic character" of the respective works. These were different and so, somewhat surprisingly, the plaintiff lost. Moral: when courts get into the realms of the "feeling and artistic character" of a work, anything can happen, *Bauman* v. *Fussell*, 1978.

(d) Changes in material form

A rather similar sort of question can arise where there is a change in the material form taken by a work; for instance, to take examples that have come before the courts, where it is suggested that a dress infringes a drawing of a dress, or a shop-front an architect's sketch of a shop-front. Clearly the two cannot be identical, in either case, but there is still a sense in which it can be said that there can be reproduction of one work by the other. Whether there is reproduction or not in any particular case is a question on which opinions are likely to differ, with the result that it is likely to be very hard to forecast what view the judge who decides the case will take.

OTHER FORMS OF INFRINGEMENT

In the case of "ordinary" literary, dramatic, musical and artistic works, reproduction (in a material form) is the primary form of infringement. For more special works there are special rules, and for "ordinary" works there are other sorts of infringement. These things are listed at the end of this chapter, and only instances will be mentioned here.

Adaptations of literary or dramatic works

It is an infringement of the copyright in a literary or dramatic work to make or reproduce an "adaptation" of it. Adaptation includes translation, and conversion into a strip-cartoon, as well as conversion of a literary into a dramatic work and vice versa. Cases about conversions and other adaptations are often very difficult, for they raise in acute form the same sort of difficulty as has already been discussed in connection with the phrase "reproduction of a substantial part of a work." Such a conversion need involve no detailed copying: a novel could be converted into a silent film, for instance (which would be "reproduction" of a dramatic adaptation, if not "reproduction" of the original work) without taking a single word—there would indeed be no words apart from occasional captions. This would be an infringement, if done without consent. If instead a sound-film were produced, it could still be an infringement, notwithstanding that the dialogue was independently written without any copying from the novel. In the same way, it has been held in one case that a ballet infringed the copyright in a short story; there could be no question of using the same words, but the ballet nevertheless "told the same story." Simply taking the bare plot does not constitute infringement in such a case; the incidents of the story must be taken too. But it is not necessary for the two works to resemble one another to the extent needed for one novel to infringe the copyright in another novel, or one play in another play. A most instructive discussion of the question of infringement of the copyright in a play by a silent film may be found in *Vane* v. *Famous Players*, 1928. We know of no case that lays down any principle as to how to decide whether a play infringes the copyright in an artistic work such as a picture; perhaps the court would look for an actual reproduction of the picture upon the stage.

Films

It may be noted that where the making of a film infringes copyright, infringement has probably already taken place before actual photographing begins: the reproduction of, or conversion into a dramatic work of, the work whose copyright is infringed, will already have happened in the preparation of the script from which the actual film is made. The actual making of the film will be a further infringement. In the same way, there was a case where a maker of gramophone records had a right to record a song but no other rights in it. He wanted the recording to be made with orchestral accompaniment, which the published version lacked; so he had a single manuscript copy prepared of the song with a suitable accompaniment. The preparation of this manuscript was held to be an infringement of copyright: arrangement or transcription of a musical work is "adaptation" and so infringement.

Issue of works to the public

It will be an act of infringement to publish a work, in the sense of issuing copies of the work to the public, without consent. This sort of infringement very seldom occurs alone, unless one is dealing with imported works. That is because publication is impossible unless copies of the work are in existence and the making of the necessary copies in this country will normally itself constitute infringement. It is also impermissible to publish a previously unpublished work, without consent. This can be important, for large damages may flow from it: in particular, the author's own chance of a successful launch may be completely spoilt by an anticipatory publication.

Performing a work in public

It is an infringement of copyright to perform a work in public without consent. (The same applies to public performance of anything close enough to a work, for its reproduction to infringe copyright). "In public" has here a rather special meaning. It refers, not to the sort of place where the performance takes place, but to the sort of audience that is present. Nor does it mean that the performance is one that anyone can attend who likes, still less that a charge must be made for admission. For this purpose, any performance is "in public" that is not restricted to members of the home circle of whoever is responsible for the performance. Guests can be present of course; there can be a very large party to see or hear the performance: but it must be a genuinely domestic affair or it will be public for copyright purposes. An amateur dramatic show by members of a Women's Institute for fellow members only; "Music While You Work" in a factory; music played so that it could be heard in the public parts of a restaurant—all these have been held to infringe copyright as "performances in public." There is an exception (for the recording copyright only—see the Note below) where a sound-recording is performed without charge as part of the amenities of a place where people sleep or as part of the activities of a non-profit-making club.

"Performance" for this purpose includes performance by means of a mechanical instrument: such as a cinematograph projector, a gramophone or wireless, a television receiver. So that showing a film in public is both "causing the film to be seen in public," involving the film copyright, and a performance in public of any play or music embodied in the film; and similarly with sound recordings. Further, although artistic works cannot be "performed" it is infringement to exhibit them on television.

If a studio performance of a play is "televised" (or a studio performance of music is broadcast), and the broadcast received in the
presence of such an audience that it is "in public," this will be a performance in public of the play or music for which whoever operates
the receiving set will be responsible: he will infringe unless he obtains
the necessary consent. In addition, the broadcaster has a separate
copyright in the broadcast: but this copyright is not infringed unless
there is a paying audience. Thus public display of a television receiver—a demonstration receiver in an ordinary shop for instance—
will give rise to an infringing performance in public if what is televised is a performance of a work; a completely impromptu
performance, however, will have no copyright but the broadcaster's
copyright, which is not infringed unless the audience pay. Thus the
interposition of a wireless link, or of a cinema camera and projector,
between a performance and its audience never prevents copyright
from being infringed; but it may give additional possibilities of
infringement.

There is a similar distinction made for tape-recordings of sound
broadcasts. It is an infringement of copyright to record a work,
whether by way of tape-recording of a broadcast or otherwise, unless
the making of the record is a "fair" dealing with the work for purposes of research or private study; see the next chapter. But the
broadcaster's copyright in the broadcast is not infringed by a record
of it made for private purposes. Since with most of the things anyone
would want to perform in public—music, plays, films, sound recordings—the copyright owners want them performed, there are well-
organised systems for selling the necessary licences. See Chapter 21.

Getting others to infringe and like cases

In accordance with ordinary rules of law, it is as much an infringement to get someone else to do an infringing act as to do it oneself. In
particular, an employer is responsible for acts of infringement committed by employees "in the course of their employment." Copyright law goes further, and makes it an infringement to authorise an
infringement: for example, an author who offers a manuscript to a
publisher to publish authorises the publisher to do so; and if the publisher sends it to a printer he authorises the printer to reproduce it. (It
is usual for publishing agreements to make the author warrant to the
publisher that the book infringes no copyright; but even without this
warranty, the ordinary law would enable the printer to recover from
the publisher, and the publisher from the author, any loss they had
suffered as a result of copyright trouble.)

"Authorising" covers other things too: any case where someone who does not control a copyright accepts a royalty for its use would be authorising the use, even though the initiative came entirely from the user. With the growth of sophisticated commercial photo-copying techniques, those who make available photo-copying facili-ties, for example in libraries, should take special care to avoid being taken to authorise the use of those facilities for the purposes of in-fringement (*Moorhouse* v. *University of New South Wales*, 1976. In practice photocopying in libraries is largely now covered by special schemes). It should be noticed, however, that merely knowing that someone else is going to infringe copyright is not inducing an in-fringement: to sell a person a copy of a play, for instance, with a warn-ing that it must not be publicly performed, can never be an infringement unless it is a copy of a pirated edition. What the buyer intends to do with it when she gets it is not the seller's affair. Such a sale without a warning is also probably safe, since a purchaser ought not to assume that she has any right to perform the play: with films the position is different, see Chapter 21. Similarly to hire out records to the public who will obviously frequently use them for home taping is not an infringement (*CBS* v. *Ames*, 1981); so also the sale of high speed tape copying machines is not an infringement in itself, though the accompanying advertising must not go so far as to incite infringe-ment or it may amount to inciting a crime (*Amstrad*, 1985).

In one respect, copyright law goes even further than that. It is in-fringement merely to permit a place of public entertainment to be used for an infringing performance, "permit" meaning merely being able to stop it and not doing so. In this case, however, if the permis-sion was not a source of profit, it is a defence that the giver had no rea-son to suppose there would be an infringement. The point of this provision is that the actual performers may well not be worth suing.

Commercial dealing

Another sort of infringement, and an important one, is commercial dealing in works which infringe copyright. Generally speaking, this covers any sort of commercial dealing (including, for instance, free distribution on any appreciable scale as well as sale); but it is limited to infringing copies. A copy which was lawfully made abroad can however infringe here, since the copyrights in different countries are separable; making dealings with it by anyone knowing the copyright position unlawful. The provisions against dealings are, generally speaking, limited to dealings by those who know or have reason to believe that the copies are infringing copies, but an innocent dealer caught with copies in his hands can usually be made to give them up, and may be liable in damages if he cannot or will not do so.

Infringing copies may be seized by the Customs on entering the country, if the copyright owner has taken the trouble to ask them to. (The traveller who brings home a book for "private and domestic" use infringes no copyright, and the seizure provisions do not apply to her; but if she later sells the book she may infringe.)

Architectural works

Architects are of course entitled to copyright in their drawings for buildings. Often there are difficulties during the course of the building works and the architect does not get paid. The question then arises as to whether the architect can prevent further work on the building until payment is made. This depends on the terms of engagement and turns on whether payment was a condition precedent to the right to use the plans or whether the architect granted the builder or plot owner a more generous licence, leaving the architect's only claim against the builder in debt. There are standard RIBA terms which govern the position (although not all architects are engaged on these terms). In general they are quite favourable to the architect.

If it is not clear in law whether or not the architect has the copyright, in practice it may be difficult for the architect to stop construction half-way. This is because, if the architect wants an interlocutory injunction to hold the position until trial, he or she will have to show loss unquantifiable in money and give a cross-undertaking in damages. Many architects will not want to risk being held to be wrong at trial, if that involves compensating the building contractor for having held up a major construction project for a number of years. One old example of architect's copyright which illustrates the problems that architects can have comes from the following case:

Example:
   In 1912 Heal & Son employed a firm of architects (Smith & Brewer) to design the famous Heals' building on Tottenham Court Road, London. There were no special terms concerning ownership of copyright but at the time the possibility of a southern extension was discussed. The building was put up and in 1935 Heal's engaged a new architect (Maufe) in connection with the extension. The extension substantially reproduced the original building. Held: the defendants had infringed the plaintiff's copyright—there was no implied licence to build a similar extension. But the damages awarded were rather modest (£150) and did not represent what the original architects could have charged for employment as architects for the extension (*Meikle* v. *Maufe*, 1941).

NOTE: "WORKS"

A list of the different sorts of "work" is given below; together with the period of copyright, and the definition of infringement, for each sort. Infringement is defined in terms of the "acts restricted by the copyright" for the sort of work concerned.

It must be remembered that a work may incorporate more than one copyright, and the various copyrights must be considered separately (there is an exception to this, mentioned below, in connection with cinematograph films).

What was said above about dealing with infringing copies applies to all sorts of work; so does what was said about "authorising"; but "permitting a place of public entertainment to be used for an infringing purpose" is infringement only of literary, dramatic or musical copyright.

1. Literary and dramatic works (Including written tables, compilations, computer programs.)

The period of copyright is 50 years from the end of the year of death of the author or publication, whichever is later. The acts restricted by the copyright are: reproduction; publication; performance in public; broadcasting; offer for sale of records of the work; adaptation or doing of the above acts to an adaptation.

"Publication," here and below, means issuing copies of a previously unpublished work to the public (*cf.* its meaning in patent law). Including a programme in a cable programme is (here and below) equivalent to broadcasting. "Adaptation," in relation to these works, means conversion from a non-dramatic to a dramatic work or vice-versa (with or without translation into another language); translation; conversion into a strip cartoon.

There are various exceptions from the definition of infringement mentioned in the next chapter; and one (not there mentioned) for recitations in public by one person of part of a work.

2. Musical works

The period of copyright, and acts restricted by it, are the same as for literary works, except that "adaptation" now means arrangement or transcription of the work. In addition to the exceptions mentioned in the next chapter, there is a provision (see Chap. 21) allowing manufacture of records of musical works for retail sale.

3. Artistic works

This term includes paintings, sculptures, drawings, engravings, photographs, works of architecture and other works of artistic craftsmanship. Etchings, lithographs, woodcuts, prints, etc., count as engravings unless they are "photographs"; whilst "photograph" includes pictures produced by processes like photography. The term of protection is 50 years from the year of death of the author. Models of buildings, as well as buildings themselves, count as architectural works.

The acts restricted by the copyright in an artistic work are: reproduction (including reproduction of a three-dimensional work in two dimensions and—subject to the special standard mentioned previously—of a two-dimensional work in three); publication; inclusion in a television programme. There are special rules as to use of artistic works as industrial designs, discussed in this chapter and Chapter 6. There are also various exceptions, discussed in the next chapter, covering the painting, photographing, etc., of sculptures permanently situated in public, of architectural works wherever situated, or of works of artistic craftmanship which both are permanently situated in a public place and also fail to qualify as artistic works under any other head. (These exceptions also cover the publication of the paintings, photographs, etc.)

4. Films and sound recordings

Sound recordings and films are copyright as such. The copyright in a film or sound recording belongs to whoever arranges for the making of it: *i.e.* usually the producer, not the cameraman or recording engineer. The term "film" is broadly defined so that (for instance) a videotape counts as a "film." Copyright in a sound recording or film expires 50 years after first release (if it is released within 50 years of being made). Or if it is not released in that time, 50 years after being made. Films and sound recordings are "released" when first shown to the public or published, or broadcast or included in a cable service.

The acts restricted by the copyright in a sound recording or film are making copies of it (or, of course, of substantial parts of it); issuing copies to the public; playing or showing it in public and broadcasting it. It is infringement to make records from the sound-track of the film (and to copy or sell the records) even though the pictures are not taken, and infringement to copy a substantial part of the picture matter even without the sound-track.

5. Typography of published books and music

There is a separate copyright in the typographical arrangement of published editions of literary, dramatic and musical works, distinct from the copyright in the works themselves. (Editions which merely reproduce the typographical arrangement of a previous edition to not count.) The copyright belongs to the publisher, and lasts for 25 years from publication. The act restricted by this copyright is making a facsimile copy. The primary function of this copyright is to protect publishers of new editions of works which are no longer copyright from pirates using up-to-date copying methods. But it also protects newspapers, for instance, from people who want to photocopy articles for sale.

6. Broadcasts and cable programmes

Copyright subsists in broadcasts, lasting for 50 years from first broadcast; this copyright restricts both re-broadcasting of the broadcast or making films and recordings of it.

NOTE: CRIMINAL OFFENCES

As well as being civilly actionable, copyright infringement is a criminal offence. The maximum penalty is two years' imprisonment and directors of
companies can be liable if the infringement was done with their consent or
connivance. Although people do not often go to prison for copyright infringement, the punishment can be severe and there are quite often stiff fines.
In a recent case, a video pirate with no previous convictions had copied 219
video cassettes. She pleaded that she was "only trying to earn a living." The
court was unmoved and, saying that it was an offence of dishonesty, gave her
two nine-month suspended sentences.

There are also provisions for Customs officials to seize infringing goods
imported into the United Kingdom upon receiving suitable notice from the
copyright owner.

20

WHAT IS NOT INFRINGEMENT

THE OWNER OF THE COPYRIGHT CANNOT CONTROL LEGITIMATE COPIES

THE copyright owner, although given large powers of control over infringement by copying and over dealings with infringing copies, has no control within a single country over legitimate copies once they have left her hands. All she can do is to ensure that such copies are not used for the purpose of other sorts of infringement. Provided she does nothing further to the work, the owner of an authorised copy can deal with it as she pleases. An instance was pointed out in Chapter 16. An ordinary business letter being copyright, the competitor who gets hold of an indiscreet letter and distributes copies of it will infringe that copyright. But provided she got hold of the letter lawfully and properly, there is nothing to stop her circulating the original amongst customers: a more troublesome proceeding perhaps but probably just as effective. So also, the purchaser of a painting will probably not own the copyright in it, but that only matters if he wants to copy it: he can sell or exhibit the original without troubling about copyright. It is only infringing copies of works that are dangerous in normal handling.

No formalities are needed for "consent" to the making of copies or of the performing of a work. The consent must be obtained before the acts to which it applies are done: in particular, a copy made without consent is an infringing copy, and a subsequent agreement with the owner of the copyright may not alter the fact. Further, unless the consent takes the form of a proper licence (such as is considered in Chap. 21), it can be withdrawn at any time. But if, at the time when a copy was made, the making had consent, then that copy is an authorised copy and the copyright owner has no more control over it.

SPECIFIC EXCEPTIONS TO THE RULES FOR INFRINGEMENT

The Copyright Designs & Patents Act lays down a number of specific exceptions to the rules for infringement. It will be observed that several of them apply only to particular categories of "works." This limitation to particular categories is important, for a court will pay strict attention to it. Some are too special to call for discussion here; they are mentioned in the Note to the preceding chapter. Some, however, are general in application.

Fair dealing for certain purposes

First, copyright will not be infringed by any fair dealing with any literary, dramatic, musical or artistic work for purposes of research or private study. "Fair" here means little more than that the treatment must be genuinely and reasonably for the purpose. For instance, an examination paper will be copyright; it will be an infringement for anyone to publish or copy and distribute the paper either before or after the examination concerned; but for a student to make a copy for his own purposes will not be an infringement. He will clearly be acting for the purpose of private study, and to take a single copy of such a work is probably "fair" in the sense of the Act. This in fact is a type of activity that the copyright law is not well adapted to prevent. On the other hand, to copy a large part of the work for private study, when the work is on sale and a copy could have been bought, probably would not be "fair" and so would be infringement. (There is a special provision, allowing works to be reproduced in the questions and answers of the actual examination.)

Similarly, fair dealing with such a work for purposes of criticism or review does not infringe. Here again it is the dealing with the work that has to be fair—not, for instance, the criticism of it. Any extract may be published, if its publication is genuinely intended to enable the reviewer to make his comments, and not to enable the reader of the review to enjoy the work concerned without buying it. Whether the whole of the work can properly be published in a review or criticism will depend upon circumstances: a whole short story could not be, but a critic of a "Penny Pool Table" was held entitled to set out the whole table in order effectively to comment upon it. But students' study notes, which reproduced substantial parts of copyright works with critical commentary, were not protected by these provisions (*Sillitoe* v. *McGraw Hill*, 1983). A review must contain an acknowledgment of the title and author of the work.

Again, there is no infringement in fair dealing with literary, musical or dramatic works for the purpose of reporting current events, either in a newspaper or magazine or in a news-reel film or broadcast (a newspaper or magazine must state the title and author of the work). What is "fair" for this purpose is less clear; in the case cited in the last chapter, about the march "Colonel Bogey," it was decided (before fair dealing was extended to news-reel films) that what was done there would not have been fair in a newspaper—that is, it would have been an infringement for a newspaper to have said: "For the benefit of those who were unable to be present yesterday, we publish the principal air of the 'Colonel Bogey' march," and then to have printed the music.

An artist re-using sketches, etc.

It is not an infringement, for the author of an artistic work who has parted with the copyright in it to make use again of preliminary sketches, models, etc., so long as he does not imitate the main design of the first work. That is to say, he may use details again, provided he does not actually copy them off the work whose copyright he has sold, but only separate details. It is of course never easy to show that an artist has infringed his own copyright, for if his style is at all individual, one picture of his is likely to be much like any other of a similar subject. It is a pity that no similar provision has been made for computer programmers, who re-use details in a rather similar way.

Photographs of works in public places

To paint, draw or photograph a building, or a piece of sculpture or suchlike work that is permanently displayed in public, is not infringement; nor is the publication of the picture. Nor is it infringement to include such a work in a film or television broadcast. There are of course restrictions on photography in many public places, but they are not copyright restrictions. The pictures themselves are of course copyright, and their reproduction would need the consent of the owner of that copyright.

Other cases

There are various provisions permitting reproduction and performance of works in the course of school lessons, and a rather limited provision permitting the publication of anthologies for school use. There are also special provisions allowing the supply by libraries of copied extracts from books and periodicals, and a provision allowing general copying, from archives, of unpublished works whose authors have been dead for more than 50 years. It is not an infringement of copyright to do any act for the purpose of parliamentary or judicial proceedings. Of course it is also not an infringement to do an act under specific statutory authority.

Time shifting

It is specifically provided that recordings made for the purpose of time-shifting are not infringements. But the recording must be made "*solely* for the purpose of enabling it to be viewed or listened to at a more convenient time." So there is nothing wrong in building up a personal film library of films shown on television. There is a range of other detailed fair-dealing provisions dealing with broadcast programmes and provision of sub-titled copies.

Computer programs

Computer programs present a special problem. There has to be a balance between the desire of creators of programs to earn revenues and the wishes of users to make back-up copies and the opportunity for other developers to create new programs which are compatible with existing ones. The result: it is not an infringement (for a lawful user of a program) to make necessary back-up copies. Nor is it an infringement to convert a program from a high level language into a low level language (*i.e.* decompile it) or copy it by doing so, provided it is necessary to decompile it to create an independent program which can be operated with the existing one and the information so obtained is not used for any other purpose. Also, it is not an infringement to do things necessary to use the program such as correcting errors in programs unless that is specifically forbidden by contract. These exceptions derive from an EC directive and they were inserted into the Copyright, Designs and Patents Act 1988 by a statutory instrument made under the European Communities Act.

Parody

It is *not* usually fair dealing to make a parody of a work. There is no statutory exception for parody and the sole test is therefore: has there been a reproduction of a substantial part of the original in making the parody?

This was graphically illustrated by a case involving a label very similar to the "SCHWEPPES" Indian tonic water label but with "SCHLURPPES" on it instead. It was intended as a joke for use on bubble bath. Schweppes did not find it funny. They sued. History does not relate whether the court was amused—in any event it granted Schweppes summary judgment.

Sauce for the gander

Although the courts are prepared to listen to a great deal of nonsense and hubris, they do not have infinite patience. The press often test it to the limit. Witness the following example which is indirectly related to fair dealing.

In 1989 Pamella Bordes, a well known public figure, was on a flight from Bali to Hong Kong. Next to her for part of the journey sat a reporter from the *Daily Express*, Mr. Frame. He did his journalistic best, asked many questions and made notes of what she said. When he got to Hong Kong, he wrote up the story. It was duly published, including some of Miss Bordes' choicest bons mots, in the *Daily Express* on April 3, 1989. The story was, in journalistic parlance, a sensation.

On the same day, April 3, *Today* came out. The first edition came out with a rather dull story about Miss Bordes. The second edition was much more juicy, including quotes from Miss Bordes, derived directly from the *Daily Express* piece.

The *Daily Express* sued for copyright infringement. Two days before the first hearing, a reporter on *Today* obtained an exclusive interview with Miss Marina Ogilvy and her boyfriend. During the interview she made certain allegations against her parents and other members of the Royal Family. That story (together with quotations from Miss Ogilvy) was published in *Today* on Monday October 9. It was described with typical journalistic modesty (as the judge observed) as "one of the most important scoops in popular journalism in modern times." The next day, the story was carried by a number of other newspapers, amongst them the *Daily Star*, another paper out of the *Daily Express* stable. A large part of the *Star* piece was taken from the *Today* article. A mirror image action was launched by the proprietors of *Today*. The court held that what was sauce for the goose was sauce for the gander: since the *Daily Express* had obtained summary judgment against *Today*, *Today* would be given summary judgment against the *Express*, even though the *Express* had raised some possible defences of fair dealing.

The public interest—control of information

Copyright can give the owner enormous control over the information—for example it can be a very effective instrument for stopping publication of embarrassing things and interlocutory injunctions are often available to restrain copyright infringement. The courts have not been too keen to prevent the free dissemination of information by restraining publication in advance, especially where it is material which the public should know about. Further, although the copyright statutes do not provide for it, there is a kind of public interest defence to infringement. Here is one example of how the public interest operates to prevent prior restraints on publication.

Example:
  Dennis Nilsen is a notorious serial killer who took a series of young men back to his flat, murdered them and dismembered their corpses. He was convicted and imprisoned for life. Central Television decided to make a documentary (called "Murder in Mind") about a new way of catching serial killers such as Nilsen, known as "offender profiling." In the course of their preparations for the programme, Central became involved in making a video of an interview with Nilsen intended (at least by the Home Office) only to be used to help in teaching the police about serial killers and advancing the techniques of offender profiling. Central obtained a copy of the videotape of the interview and wanted to show a short extract from it on television as part of their documentary. The Home Secretary objected, claiming copyright in the film and breach of an agreement not to use the material. The case was arguable but it was not possible to say at the interlocutory stage who was right. Central argued that it would be in the public interest for the extract to be shown since it would help to warn people of how "normal" serial killers could appear. The courts agreed that there was an issue of public interest and that Central should not be restrained by interlocutory injunction from showing the extract (*Home Secretary* v. *Central Television*, 1993).

The Right to Reproduce, Subject to Royalties

In certain cases, works may be reproduced without consent provided royalties are paid to the owner of the copyright; but this is a topic belonging to Chapter 21.

21

DEALINGS IN COPYRIGHT

INTRODUCTION

THE right given to an author by the Copyright Act, of preventing other people from reproducing her works, is of very little value in itself: for the main problem in almost every case is to get herself into a position where anyone wants to reproduce the works at all. That problem is outside the scope of this book. Once it has been solved however a whole group of legal questions arise: not only formal problems of transfer of copyright, but various other questions, as to the terms on which reproduction shall take place, whether the money is to be paid to the author or the Inland Revenue, and so on. It is with questions of this type that the present chapter is concerned.

FORMAL PROBLEMS

On transfers of copyright

Copyright can be freely transferred, either as a whole or for a particular field: thus the film rights in a novel, for instance, or the performing rights in a play, can be transferred separately from the right of printing and publishing. The copyright in any country outside the United Kingdom can—so far as English law is concerned—be dealt with separately from the United Kingdom rights. But the transfer must be in writing; and a transfer is not the same as an agreement to transfer. Consider for instance the common case of a book or article commissioned by a publisher for a lump sum, on the terms that the publisher is to get the copyright. Perhaps there is a written agreement to that effect. Even so, however, the agreement will not then and there transfer the copyright: for it will be entered into before the work is created, and so there will be no copyright then in existence for it to transfer. If the agreement purports to assign the copyright, and there is nothing else wrong, and the agreement is signed on behalf of the prospective owner of the copyright, the effect will be that the copyright belongs to the publisher when it comes into existence. If

165

not, the position will be that the author owns the copyright, but he has agreed that the publisher shall have it. Some publishers do, some do not, demand an actual assignment in such cases, though all could do so if they wished. For most purposes, the position is of course the same as if the copyright had been transferred; but if any sort of dispute arises, the difference will become important. If the copyright is infringed, for instance, and the publisher wishes to sue the infringer, either the publisher must get a written assignment of the copyright, together with the right to sue for past infringements, or the action will have to be brought in the author's name, though the publisher must pay for it and will be entitled to any damages that may be recovered. Or again, suppose there is a dispute as to who is going to have the copyright, and the author (thinking herself entitled to do so, or even acting dishonestly) sends it to a second publisher who knows nothing of the agreement with the first, the second sale will be effective: the author as actual owner of the copyright could validly sell it, and the only remedy of the first publisher is to sue her for breaking her contract. (If the second publisher knew of the agreement, or even if circumstances were such that he ought to have found out about it, then he will be bound by it.)

This distinction between selling and agreeing to sell runs right through the English law of property; confusing as it is, there are many problems that cannot be understood unless it is borne in mind. In connection with the sale of a house, or something like that, few people forget that until the house has been formally conveyed to its new owner it is not hers; but with intangible property like copyright this is not so easy to remember. There is a reported case for instance of the reconstruction of a company, where the old company's assets included a copyright of great value that was never actually transferred to the new company; the omission being discovered only after the old company had been dissolved. The difficulty could be, and was, overcome with the aid of the High Court; but that sort of things costs time and money. Few companies would wind themselves up without for instance handing over the land on which their factory was built.

Foreign formalities

Where foreign copyrights are concerned, any transfer must conform to the legal requirements of the country concerned; some countries demand more and some less in the way of ceremony when property is transferred, and although an assignment valid by English law will usually suffice if it is made in England, it is seldom wise to rely on this. In some countries copyrights may be registered, and failure to register may involve inconvenience. In countries like America, which are very strict about monopolies (as well as having copyright laws differing from ours) it is always unwise to try to do without native legal advice. Of course, those who are much involved in copyright matters (film companies and music publishers, for instance) have rule-of-thumb methods for handling foreign copyright problems which seem usually to work well enough.

On licensing

An owner of copyright who does not want to transfer it outright may license it: that is to say, may grant to someone else the right to do acts that would normally infringe that copyright. Again, the licence should be in writing; and here also there is a distinction that must be watched—that between a licence and a mere consent to the doing of certain acts. There is never any infringement involved in reproducing a copyright work, if the owner of the copyright consents; but a true licence carries with it a right of property in a way that a mere consent does not. Thus a true licence can give rights enforceable against the owner himself (in case he should change his mind) or against anyone to whom he sells the copyright, whilst an exclusive licensee can sue infringers. A mere consent on the other hand can be withdrawn by the copyright owner, or overridden by a sale of the copyright, leaving the other party with nothing except (possibly) a right to sue for breach of contract. Licences require no special formalities in English law.

CONTRACTS RELATING TO COPYRIGHTS

Apart from the points already mentioned in this chapter, dealings in copyright are entirely a matter for contract—that is to say, those concerned may make what rules they please. What has happened in relation to any particular copyright must consequently be deduced from such agreements, formal or informal, as the parties have made; this may be a matter of very great difficulty. It should in particular be assumed that any agreement drawn up by business people will prove difficult for lawyers (including judges) to sort out; for lawyers and business people have quite different ideas both as to the way they use language and as to the sort of things that agreements ought to provide for. It is however possible to lay down a few general rules as to what the position is likely to be if the parties have said nothing definite to the contrary.

Implied terms

In all cases it has to be remembered that the law is very chary of reading into agreements terms that the parties have not actually stated. The rule is: such terms will only be implied if the agreement cannot be effective without them, so that there can be no doubt that if when the contract was made the parties had been asked whether this was what they wanted, they would both have said "Yes, of course." For example, if there is a sale of a copyright work of art, such as a picture, the copyright will not be transferred with the work unless the parties agree that it shall. This is obvious in the case of a work with many copies, like a coloured print; it is not so obvious in the case of something like a painting of which only the original exists. But if the parties are silent as to the copyright, the law will not assume that they meant to transfer it unless it is clear that this must have been so. In the case, say, of a sale of a painting to a maker of Christmas cards, if both parties knew that he meant to make a Christmas card of it, it will be clear that they must have meant that he should have some right to reproduce the painting; but even then, it does not necessarily follow that he must have the ownership of the copyright rather than a licence to reproduce. In any event, unless there is something in writing, he will get merely a contractual right to have the copyright assigned to him or a licence granted to him, as the case may be.

Where works are made to order

Works made to order present a special problem (see Chap. 18). It will often be clear (if not expressly stated) that the parties meant the copyright to be transferred to the person giving the order; a term in their agreement to that effect will then be implied. For instance, where a publisher commissions a book for a lump sum payment, even if nothing is said about copyright it will normally be assumed that the publisher is meant to have it. The author is not an employee, so as to make the publisher the first owner of the copyright: this is shown by the fact that the publisher cannot tell her how to write the book but must take it as the author thinks it should be written. Nevertheless, for a lump sum payment the publisher presumably expected to get the whole thing, copyright and all. (But remember that there will only be an agreement to transfer the copyright to the publisher, not an actual transfer, unless a signed agreement says it is a transfer.) On the other hand if payment is to be by royalty there will be no reason to suppose that the publisher is necessarily to have more than a licence to publish; and in the case of an architectural work for instance, even if specially commissioned, the only term as to copyright which will be implied into the contract is a licence to the architect's client to erect the buildings contracted for in accordance with the drawings. The architect will therefore keep his copyright. A clear case the other way was of a man who was commissioned to do the choreography for a ballet: clearly the copyright must have been intended to be transferred to the man who commissioned the work, for without that copyright he would not have a complete ballet.

Where a publisher agrees to publish an author's work

There are cases however where it is clear that the parties must have intended to provide for quite a number of matters they have said nothing about. For instance, an author may send the manuscript of a book to a publisher and the publisher agree to publish it, and nothing else is said at all. In that case the law will imply, grudgingly, the bare minimum of terms to complete the contract. The publisher has a licence to publish an edition of the book, but that is all: the author of course keeps the ownership of the copyright. The publisher must pay the author a reasonable royalty: not necessarily the royalty he usually pays, rather the sort of royalty an ordinary publisher would normally pay for that sort of book. The publisher must publish an edition of the book, of reasonable size having regard to all the circumstances, within a reasonable time. A reasonable time for publishing a book in these days will be many months, and there would certainly be no obligation upon the publisher to hurry unduly; but he must not deliberately delay. He must not for instance, as a publisher once did, deliberately delay publication so as to enable a rival to scoop the Christmas market with a book on the same subject—in return of course for a share of the profits on his rival's book. Finally he is not entitled to publish the book under someone else's name as author: the position would however be different if he had bought the copyright outright, then he could probably deal with the work as he pleased, subject to any moral rights (see Chap. 23).

In the same way, if a manuscript is sent to the editor of a periodical the editor may publish it, and must pay at reasonable rates. His usual rates will usually do, and will certainly do if the author has taken them before: but a periodical which usually pays unusually low rates should tell new authors about them before publication, or it may find that the court considers them unreasonable. The editor of a periodical is not entitled to publish in book form manuscripts sent to him for periodical publication, without the author's consent.

Bequests of copyright works

In one case the Copyright Act itself creates a presumption that copyright goes with the property in the actual work: where an artistic work, or the manuscript of a literary, musical or dramatic work, is bequeathed by a will which does not mention the copyright. (Of course, this only applies so far as the testator owned the copyright when he died.)

Sales of part of a copyright

The same sort of considerations arise when a copyright is partially sold; but here the position tends to be clearer, for the parties must have said something about that they intend shall happen; and all the lawyers have to decide is what the parties' words mean. (The answer may surprise the parties, but that often happens to those who are insufficiently explicit in the first place.) Thus the sale of the performing rights in a play or a song will not pass the right to make films or records of the work, unless there is some special reason why the parties must have meant this to be so; but it will pass the right to prevent any film or record of the work being shown or played in public. This will be vital in the case of a play to be made into a film, which is almost certainly intended for public exhibition (unless perhaps it is meant solely for export to a country where either there is no copyright or the performing right has not been sold); but it will be less important to the maker of a record. Records as normally sold are in fact not licensed for a public performance, and every UK record at least bears a notice to that effect.

The Performing Right Society and Phonographic Performance Ltd.

What actually happens with musical copyrights is that the performing rights in published music are handed over to a licensing and royalty collection body called the Performing Right Society. The broadcasting, performing and diffusion rights in sound recordings go likewise to a collecting body called Phonographic Performance Ltd., set up by the recording companies. In the case of films including previously published music, the film company buys a licence to include the music in the film (there are standard arrangements for this), but does not have authority to license public performance of it. The cinema has a standard Performing Right Society licence which covers that.

The film distributor, in effect, warrants that an exhibitor will have no copyright trouble, provided his cinemas have Performing Right Society licences (that is to say, the film company is expected to look after performing rights in any book or play the film is made from, but not performing rights in music except music specially written for the film). The actual agreements used in the film industry tend to be rather incomprehensible, but custom has established what they are supposed to mean.

People wanting to use records, tapes or CDs for public performance (*e.g.* for use in village halls) go to the two societies and obtain standard licences: one covering the copyright in music, one covering that in the recording. There is a Copyright Tribunal with power to see that the standard licences are not unreasonable.

It should be noted that the control of licensing by the Copyright Tribunal is of great importance, especially in the entertainment industry where collective licensing bodies are commonplace. In 1988, the Monopolies and Mergers Commission said that collective licensing bodies were by their nature monopolistic and "it is widely accepted that appropriate controls are needed to ensure that they do not abuse their market power." There have been such controls for some time—prior to the 1988 Act there was the Performing Right Tribunal which exercised similar powers. The 1988 Act changed its name and widened its jurisdiction considerably. As well as setting terms for collective licensing schemes, the Tribunal can, for example, determine royalties for the rental right, grant certain consents on behalf of performers in certain circumstances, and settle the terms of licences of right, if the Monopolies and Mergers Commission determines that the copyright owner is engaging in anti-competitive practices contrary to the public interest.

Where the ownership of the manuscript and copyright is in different hands

A case similar to overlapping copyrights arises where the owner of an unpublished manuscript does not own the copyright in it. He cannot publish it without the copyright owner's consent, but then the copyright owner cannot get at the manuscript without his consent: so that again an intending publisher must come to terms with both.

Publishing agreements

Two odd points relating to publishing agreements deserve notice. Such agreements often contain a clause requiring the author to offer her next book (or next so many books) to the same publisher. This is a perfectly legitimate clause for a contract to contain, and can be enforced: a court will grant an injunction not only to prevent the author disposing of those books elsewhere, but also to prevent another publisher, who took those books although he knew about the agreement, from publishing them. On the other hand, an agreement to write a number of further books would not be enforceable by injunction: injunctions are not given to compel the performance of personal services.

The second point is more difficult. Suppose the author, not being under any obligation to offer his next book to the same publisher, writes another on the same subject and offers it to a second publisher, who publishes it and so spoils the market for the first: has the first publisher any remedy? Or suppose the publisher puts out a second book on the same subject at the same time, and so spoils the first author's sales: has the author any remedy? The answer will of course depend on what the publishing agreement says, and since the publisher will very likely have drawn it up it will probably protect him against the author but not the author against him. If the agreement is altogether silent on the subject, it seems fairly clear that in an ordinary case the author would have no remedy; probably the publisher would have none either, but this is not quite so clear.

Literary agents

It is usual for established authors at least to employ literary agents to place their books and deal with the various forms of copyright arising from them. Here again, the rights of the author and his agent as against each other are what they have agreed them to be when the agent took the job. It should be remembered however that as against the outside world, the agent's powers to deal on behalf of his principal will in effect be those that such agents usually have. The author can, if she likes and the agent is willing, make special terms and place special restrictions on the agent's authority; but the special terms and restrictions will have no effect against third parties who do not know of them.

Manuscripts sent for advice

It is not unusual for authors who are not established to send their works to their more successful colleagues for comment, advice, and assistance in placing with publishers or producers. The rights of the author in such a case are clear. The person she sends her manuscript to must not of course publish it (though he may be expected to show it to one or two colleagues), nor may he copy from it: but he is under no obligation to take any particular care of it, and if it gets lost or damaged the author should not complain.

TAXATION AND AUTHORS

The question of tax upon author's earnings, important as it is, can be dealt with here only very briefly. The position is broadly this. Any author who makes a business or profession of writing or composing, or anyone who makes a business of dealing in copyrights, must pay income tax on the whole profits of that business, whether they are received in the form of royalties or of lump-sum payments. Those who do not make a business of it, like casual authors or people who happen to have come into possession of an odd copyright, must pay income tax on receipts if they are income but not if they are capital. It does not necessarily follow that royalties are income, though they usually are; still less does it follow that lump-sum payments are capital. The test is more or less this: was there a valuable asset, and has it been converted into money (in which case the proceeds of conversion will be capital) or has it been used as a source of profit—as an income-bearing investment, so to speak? If it has, that profit will be income. A sale of an existing copyright, by someone who has never written a book before, whether for a single payment or annual payments, may be capital, and not taxable by income tax; on the other hand a royalty of so much a copy on the sales of a book is almost certainly income, even if it is paid as a lump sum when the agreement is made. If a work is commissioned, the payment is almost certain to be received as income whatever form it takes: for essentially it is payment for services, not the sale of any asset. It will be seen that the author of a really successful work will find some difficulty in arranging her affairs so as to avoid paying out in one or two years of extremely high income, most of what she gets for it. However, such an author can, to a reasonable extent, "spread" out (for tax purposes) payments she receives, over a longer period.

22

CONFIDENCE

INTRODUCTION

THE present chapter deals with a matter in some way akin to copy-right (though it does not depend on Acts of Parliament): not the right to stop others from reproducing a work, but to stop them making use of the information contained in it. This is a job which the ownership of copyright will seldom do. Thus it will be recalled that a purchaser of a book is entitled to read it and let anyone else read it, and even to recite bits of it in public to anyone who will listen. No limitation by way of limited licence can be imposed by the owner of the copyright if the copy is an authorised copy; even if the copy is not authorised all the copyright owner can do is to insist upon the handing over of the book to him—what he cannot do by virtue of his ownership of the copyright is to prevent readers of the book making use of what they learnt by reading it.

The sort of problems dealt with in this chapter generally, although not always, arise in commercial matters: with the inventor who shows the invention to others before patents have been granted or even (inventors are not always cautious people) before he has applied for patents at all; the manufacturer who supplies manufacturing drawings and specifications to a sub-contractor; the merchant who gives the names and addresses of customers to the manufacturer so that they can be supplied direct. In all cases of this sort, what the person who supplied the information really wants is to stop the recipient of the information from using it except for the purpose for which it was given. A mere right to stop the recipient from making copies, which is given by copyright, is useful but is not enough.

THE ACTION FOR BREACH OF CONFIDENCE

The general rule

The right needed by a supplier of confidential information is given by the law, but only in certain circumstances and subject to certain exceptions. The general rule has been put in the following way, namely, that a recipient of confidential information may not use that information without the consent of the person he got it from (*Saltman Engineering* v. *Campbell Engineering*, 1948). Another way in which the rule has been expressed is that a plaintiff who sues for breach of confidence must show three things: first, that the information has the necessary quality of confidence about it; secondly, that the information was imparted in circumstances importing an obligation of confidence; and thirdly, that there was an unauthorised use made of that information (*Coco* v. *Clark*, 1969). The judge who decided the latter case thought that it was possible that the plaintiff would also have to show that he was personally prejudiced by the unauthorised use of the information, but did not decide the point.

When is information confidential?

(a) Circumstances giving rise to a relationship of confidence

These can be shortly stated: a person can be prevented from misusing information given to him if, when he receives it, he has agreed, expressly or impliedly, to treat it as confidential. This does not mean that there has to be a formal agreement, although of course having such an agreement helps to make the position clear to everyone (which is why the cases which are fought are mostly concerned with situations where the parties did not make it clear that their relationship was confidential from the outset). What the judges do in cases where there is no express agreement is to look at all the circumstances surrounding the relationship between the parties. If it appears that the parties cannot have intended the information to be given freely, then it was given in confidence. A lot may depend upon how the judge feels about the way the defendant behaved. If information is given for a particular purpose, it is easily inferred that the parties intended the information to be used only for that purpose. A few examples will make the point clearer.

In *Seager* v. *Copydex*, 1967 an inventor had discussed an invention of his with the defendant company with a view to their taking it up. In the course of the discussion he mentioned the idea behind another invention he had in mind. Although the company did not take up the first invention, they later came out with a version of the second, even using the name which the inventor had given it. The Court of Appeal thought the defendant must have taken the inventor's idea, albeit subconsciously, and that the relationship between the parties must have been confidential since the inventor could not be supposed to have been giving the information freely; it was given merely for the purpose of interesting the defendant in his ideas. Similarly in *Fraser* v. *Thames TV*, 1982 three actresses had given to a television company, the idea of a soap opera relating the adventures of an all girl rock band. They contemplated that they would take the starring roles but the TV company stole the idea and had to pay heavy damages for breach of confidence.

Again, in *Ackroyds* v. *Islington Plastics*, 1962 the defendants had been under contract to manufacture plastic "swizzle sticks" (things for getting those nasty bubbles out of champagne) for the plaintiffs. The plaintiffs had supplied the defendants for this purpose with information and with a special tool. It was held that the defendants could not use either the information or the tool for the purpose of manufacturing swizzle sticks for themselves: both had been handed over only for the purpose of helping them manufacture for the plaintiffs.

One other example shows that the law of confidence, although mostly finding its application in the commercial field, is perfectly general. In *Argyll* v. *Argyll*, 1965 the then Duchess of Argyll sued to prevent the Duke from supplying to a Sunday newspaper (and to prevent the Sunday newspaper from publishing) what the Duke had said to her in confidence during their marriage, which had ended in divorce a little earlier. The judge said that the marriage relationship was in its nature confidential and that the obligations of confidence continued after the marriage had ended. The interlocutory injunctions against publication of the "Spycatcher" diaries in the United Kingdom were based on breach of confidence by Peter Wright although the House of Lords said that the crown may also be entitled to copyright in them, *Att. Gen.* v. *Guardian Newspapers*, 1990.

(b) The effect of marking things "confidential"

We have said that the test of confidentiality is the express or implied intention of the parties. It follows that marking a document "confidential" will not necessarily make it so, if the person who receives it does not know, and has no reason to expect, that it is to be confidential. If you see a book advertised for sale and send up the money and get a copy of the book back, the book is already yours before you unpack it or look at it. It may turn out to be highly confidential and labelled so, but that makes no difference: you did not agree not to disclose its contents when you offered to buy it and you need not agree now. On the other hand, if the book is stated in the advertisement to be confidential, only for your personal use, then in replying to the advertisement you agree to keep it as confidential and must keep to your contract—even if on investigation the book turns out to be something you could buy at any bookstall or—as in one decided case—an explanation of a system for betting on horse-races according to the phases of the moon.

(c) Confidence and contract

Where parties are in a contractual relationship they often provide for obligations of confidence in express terms. Thus normally no scientist will be employed by the research department of a company unless she agrees to keep the company information secret even after she leaves the company. But even where there is no such express obligation, the relationship between the parties may of its nature give rise to obligations of confidence: as in the "swizzlestick" case mentioned above, or in *Robb* v. *Green*, 1895 where an ex-employee was restrained from using a list of his old employer's customers for his own benefit. The point is that the law of confidence exists apart from the law of contract, but when obligations of confidence exist there is usually some contractual relationship between the parties.

(d) What happens where the information becomes public knowledge

Suppose that by the time the action comes to trial the information concerned has been either wholly or partly made available to the public. What then?

At first sight it would seem absurd that a defendant should be under any restriction in using information which is public knowledge. But things are not so simple: a defendant may obtain a considerable advantage from information which, when it was supplied to him, was confidential but which has now become public knowledge—one judge expressed this sort of situation vividly by saying that such a defendant was using the information as a "springboard for activities detrimental to the plaintiff."

At present the law upon this subject is not clear. On the one hand it has been held that a man who lets all the information be disclosed by publication of his patent specification can no longer prevent ex-employees from revealing that information. On the other hand it is also clear that the courts are willing to give some relief to a plaintiff who shows that the defendant has obtained an unfair advantage by using the plaintiff's confidential information as a "springboard" even when the information has later become public. The courts say that, in such cases, although it is true that the information was available from public sources, the defendant did not get it from them, but got it from the "tainted source" of the plaintiff's confidential disclosure to him. Once a defendant is under the suspicion that he has used a "tainted source" he may find himself in difficulty. It may then be no use his saying "Look, I know I had dealings with the plaintiff in the past which were confidential, but I developed this machine by myself and here are my plans to prove it." The court may still feel he got the idea from the plaintiff and find a breach of confidence. *Seager* v. *Copydex* is just such a case. Another example is afforded by the manufacturer who has a list of the customers of the merchant for whom he makes goods. In the sort of field where this point is most likely to arise it may be that anyone could compile a pretty good list of customers and potential customers from trade directories and the like. Nevertheless, let such a manufacturer once show a disposition to take unfair advantage of his position and he may find himself forbidden to approach those customers at all. In some recent cases judges have taken a middle course—granting an injunction to last long enough to destroy the head start gained by the defendant's breach of confidence.

The difficulties in this concept of the "springboard" case are well described in the judgment in *Coco* v. *Clark*.

Remedies

The remedies for a breach of confidence are much the same as those granted for the infringement of the other rights discussed in this book (see Chap. 1). Thus injunctions can be, and often are, awarded, together with damages or accounts of profits. In some cases the court will not award an injunction but will award damages only. This occurred in *Seager* v. *Copydex* where, since the information was, at the time of the action, publicly known and the plaintiff's information was only a part of the information being used by the defendants, an injunction was thought to be inappropriate and damages enough to compensate the plaintiff. In fact there followed a dispute as to the way in which damages should be calculated and the matter had to go to the Court of Appeal again upon this question (*Seager* v. *Copydex*, 1969). The court held that damages should be paid upon the market value of the information, which depended upon how important it was: whether, for example, it was inventive enough to support a patent, or was merely the sort of information which could have been supplied by any expert.

Interlocutory injunctions

If the plaintiff acts quickly enough he will in a suitable case be granted an interlocutory injunction: where the information concerned is not yet public, for instance, to preserve the status quo while the case is fought. But in "springboard" cases it seems that the courts are unwilling to grant such injunctions, partly because the questions of fact as to exactly how much of the information used by the defendant was taken from the plaintiff and how much the defendants got for themselves are too difficult to resolve without hearing all the evidence, and partly because, in such cases, the plaintiff may in the end, if he wins, receive only damages. *Coco* v. *Clark*, 1969 is an example of such a refusal. (But note that the judge, whilst refusing the interlocutory injunction, thought that the defendants ought, pending the trial, to pay a potential royalty into a bank account so that if the plaintiff eventually won the action, he would be safeguarded, and an undertaking to this effect was given to the court.)

Suing third parties

If the owner of the information is able to act before it has been disclosed to any third party, then an injunction preventing disclosure should be all he needs to protect it. If it has already been passed on to a third party, an injunction will not be much good unless it binds the third party too. Anyone who receives information that he knows (or ought to know) reached him through a breach of confidence has a duty not to use or disclose it, and the court will in a proper case grant an injunction to enforce that duty. Thus in the *Argyll* case mentioned above, not only the Duke was placed under an injunction but also the Sunday newspaper which was going to print the information. Similarly in "Spycatcher."

The exact limits to the circumstances in which third parties can be sued are not yet fully worked out because there have not been many cases on the subject. However, the law is probably that where someone pays for the information in good faith then he cannot be stopped from using it. It would be different if he acted in bad faith (for example where a company has bought information from someone it knew to be an industrial spy or an employee of another company) and it may be different if he does not pay for it.

Problems of proof

From what has been said, it might be thought that the law gave enough protection to confidential information to make disclosure of it perfectly safe. Any such idea would be entirely wrong. As always, neither the general law nor even a carefully drawn contract is any real protection against dishonesty. The function of these things—of a proper contract especially—is to make it clear, amongst honest parties to a transaction, just what they may and may not do.

If a would-be plaintiff does come up against a rogue then she will find it difficult to prove her case. The burden will lie on her to show she gave the rogue confidential information in circumstances giving rise to a bond of confidence and that the rogue is using such information. In some cases the would-be plaintiff will not even know that the rogue is using the information. For example, suppose a company learns from an employee of another company that a particular line of research has been tried and found useless. This will save the first company from trying that line, but the company from whom the information was "taken" will have very little chance of proving that the other company acted in breach of confidence. When it comes to information passed on to third parties the problems of proof grow even harder.

Where the action will not lie

(a) "No confidence in a guilty secret"

Since the action for breach of confidence is founded originally upon what is fair, the courts will not grant a remedy if the information which the defendant threatens to reveal or use is something which ought not, in conscience, to be protected. Thus, for example, in *Initial Towel Services* v. *Putterill*, 1967 the plaintiffs failed to obtain interlocutory injunctions against an ex-employee and a daily newspaper when the ex-employee alleged that the information he was giving to the newspaper showed that the plaintiffs had been a party to a secret arrangement to keep prices up, contrary to the Restrictive Trade Practices Act.

(b) Public policy

There are some cases where, as a matter of public policy, agreements for confidence will not be enforced. The most important of these is in relation to skilled employees who leave their firm and propose to enter employment in the same field, perhaps with a rival manufacturer. The court will enforce covenants preventing the ex-employee from working for the competitor, provided that the covenant is not too broad in terms of the geographical area to which it extends and the time for which it operates. The court goes further, and, whether or not there is a covenant in restraint of trade in his contract of employment, will prevent an employee or ex-employee from disclosing the industrial or commercial secrets of his employer. What the court will not do, however, is to prevent him from using the general skill and knowledge (as opposed to confidential information) which he has acquired by reason of his employment. Obviously the distinction between these two is a hard one to draw in some cases, but it must be drawn, for otherwise skilled employees would never be able to change their jobs. So important do the courts regard the ability of a skilled person to do his or her job that even an express agreement seeking to bind the employee not to use such general knowledge will be held invalid—although that does not mean that the employee will be free to disclose company secrets.

The position of directors deserves special mention: any information obtained by a director by virtue of his office is, in effect, held on trust for the company, and must only be used for the purposes of the company. Since the directors are responsible for the conduct of the business of the company, it is seldom open to them to say that they were not told and did not realise that the information acquired was confidential.

(c) The duty of confidence must be owed to the plaintiff

In *Fraser* v. *Evans*, 1969 the plaintiff sought to restrain by interlocutory injunction publication in a newspaper of parts of a confidential report he had prepared for the Greek Government. It was held that although the report was confidential and although the copyright belonged to the plaintiff, he could not succeed. He failed as to infringement of copyright since it appeared very likely that, at the trial, a defence of fair dealing (see Chap. 20) would succeed; and he failed as to breach of confidence because the report belonged to the Greek Government and not to him. Only the person to whom the duty of confidence is owed can sue to enforce it.

SALES OF "KNOW-HOW"

It is not uncommon, in these days, for know-how to be treated as an article of commerce—to be sold outright, like any other property, or to be handed over on terms like those of a patent licence. Even an actual patent licence may often turn out, in reality, to be largely a dealing in know-how—it is often the know-how that is worth the money, rather than the more-or-less dubious monopoly given by any patent. This sort of transaction presents no very great difficulty in the ordinary case where both parties are honest. The agreements governing such transactions deal in detail with the degree of "confidence" to be attached to the information handed over, and especially with the position after the agreement comes to an end. This sort of transaction is rather outside the scope of the present chapter, which is more concerned with cases in which there is no express agreement laying down conditions as to confidence.

The Need for Agreements

It is always better to have questions of confidence properly covered by agreement, than to leave them to implications of the general law. Consider once again the case of a manufacturer trying out an invention. Everything may go well, in which case there will be no difficulty. But suppose the inventor's ideas turn out in the end to be more-or-less unworkable. The manufacturer may then drop the whole scheme; but suppose that in the course of finding out that the invention will not work he finds out what is wrong, and so becomes able to make something that will work. What is to be the position then? The manufacturer, especially if he has paid for the right to have first go at the invention, will feel that he has taken from the inventor nothing he has not paid for, that the new ideas are his own and that he owes the inventor nothing. The inventor will probably feel that the manufacturer is either merely being difficult, or merely making undesirable alterations in the original scheme so as to get out of paying a proper royalty. If a fight is to be avoided, there ought to be an agreement which will make it clear exactly what the manufacturer is entitled to keep if he rejects the original invention, and just exactly when a royalty or purchase price is in the end to be payable. Making detailed agreements is not a sure way of avoiding litigation. One of the longest commercial arbitrations ever was about a confidential information agreement (dealing with the manufacture of glass) that went wrong.

DIFFICULT CASES

Of course, there are difficulties no agreement can provide against; especially as neither inventors nor manufacturers are always as sensible and co-operative as they might be. For instance, if a manufacturer can be interested at all in an invention put up to him, the reason is likely to be that the problem it sets out to solve is one he knew of and had even been dabbling at himself. His reaction to seeing an outsider's proposal is likely to be that he rejects it but is encouraged to go back to his own ideas and make them work—perhaps with a bit of help from the alternative proposals that the outside inventor has put to him. Inevitably, in most such cases, the inventor will be convinced that the manufacturer has "really" stolen his invention, and the manufacturer will be convinced that he has merely pursued (as he "really" always meant to) his own previous line of development. They will never agree on the facts, and may have to ask a court to decide between them. If a proper agreement is made between them, before the invention is disclosed, this should serve to limit the range of the dispute, and so will save time, costs and some bitterness, if nothing else; but even so a dispute may be inevitable. It is worth examining in some detail the factors that make disputes so difficult to avoid in many matters of confidence.

The instance just given suggests one factor: that much information seems very much more valuable to the person giving it than to the person listening. Another factor is well illustrated by the case suggested earlier, of a merchant who lets suppliers know the names of his customers. The real trouble here is, that the merchant's position is inherently a risky one; sooner or later, it will pay his suppliers or his customers to cut him out, and what seems to them an ordinary change in business procedure will look to him like dirty work. He will look on a list of customers or suppliers as something of great value, since to him it is; but to others, such a list is worth precisely what it would cost to pay a person to compile it from business directories. So often what really matters is not some trade secret but just trade habits that nobody bothers to alter. The same thing can happen with industrial know-how: the difference between making something well and making it badly can be a matter of secret knowledge, but is more often a matter of skilled management and skilled labour. If a good person gets a job somewhere else at higher pay, and her new employer's products jump ahead in quality, it is easy to assume that some secret has gone with her; but the odds are that secrets played very little part in the matter. So one gets a sort of typical case, where the defendant has been rather careless over the plaintiff's confidence, not thinking it mattered much; and the plaintiff is over-suspicious, not realising that any competent person in the defendant's position could do the job without anybody's secrets. Both parties are sure they are 90 per cent. in the right: and the result can easily be litigation, whose outcome will be anyone's guess. There are people who deliberately set out to steal their employer's secrets; but most litigation, in this field as in any other, is between people who just did not think enough.

Of course a lot of litigation about commercial confidentiality is pursued to nip in the bud any potential competition from ex-employees. Thus a lot of plaintiffs have succeeded in doing a great deal of damage to (quite honest) ex-employee defendants by getting things like *Anton Piller* orders against them (see Chap. 2). For many years, the courts were concerned about dishonest defendants walking off with their ex-employer's secrets. Some judges would hand out the most draconian orders (originally intended to deal with wholly crooked video pirates) almost on the nod. Now there is increasing concern about over-aggressive plaintiffs using the courts to put these kinds of defendants out of business. This is important, since the costs of litigation are such that clearing one's name and getting an unjustified order discharged is often a serious drain on a new business's resources.

NOTE: A BRIEF EXCURSION INTO A DRY DEBATE

Lawyers are fond of disputation—never more than when nothing is at stake. One instance of this is a row which has smouldered along in the pages of academic journals for about a hundred years concerning the legal nature of confidential information. It is one thing to say that the law will prevent people from taking the fruits of breaches of confidence, it is quite another to work out (as a matter of legal theory) why such protection should exist in the first place. After all, there must be some basis for creating a liability. There are (essentially) three views.

The first (and probably the most ancient) is property based. This holds that confidential information is a kind of property just like any other which can be transferred and is protected by an action in essence similar to conversion of goods or trespass. But, confidential information does not have one important incident of other personal property—you are not guilty of theft if you steal it (see, *e.g. Oxford* v. *Moss*, 1978 student "stealing" examination paper).

The second is the contractualist view. This holds that confidential information is protected because of a kind of contract, express or implied. But purely contractualist theories of legal liability are out of favour at present. In any event this theory does not really make room for the notion of stopping a third party, who has got hold of the information from the impartee, from using or disclosing it.

The third is a rather more nebulous approach based on the enforcement of equitable obligations of confidence. This is the approach which is currently dominant. Thus, there is said to be an obligation of confidence based on "good faith" and although the courts may not be able to define precisely when the principles will be invoked, they know a case for their application when they see one.

In practice, the inability clearly to articulate a basis or framework for protection is not as serious as it might be in other cases. There are usually so many other uncertainties of fact and law in confidential information cases (such as whether the information has the necessary quality of confidence about it) that adding a little disquiet about the basis for granting relief does not make too much difference.

The important underlying point which this debate highlights is that monopolies protected in virtue of the proprietorship of or control over confidential information are only regulated by the courts—obligations of "good faith" are rather powerful and flexible legal instruments in the hands of judges. Now and again there are official stirrings about statutory provisions—the Law Commission produced an influential report some years ago, but nothing has been done.

23

MORAL RIGHTS

Moral rights have nothing to do with morals. They are special rights conferred by the Copyright Designs and Patents Act 1988 and are intended to give creative people a sense of artistic control over their copyright works. The name comes from the French ("droit moral")—the French and Germans have traditionally been much more interested in these kinds of rights. The main moral rights are unlike a lot of the rest of intellectual property; they are about Creativity and Art, not economics—so the orthodox theory goes anyway.

Artists and writers are often (and rightly) concerned about two things: fame and the "artistic integrity" of their works. Of course, both of these can be of commercial importance too; fame is usually swiftly followed by profit. Much of the popular appeal of intellectual property is derived from images of the starving (balding and bearded?) inventor in a garret or impecunious artists eking out a living from a bare paint-splashed studio. Moral rights are inspired by a slightly different popular image: the artist whose creative genius goes unrecognised while his or her works are sold on every street corner; or the writer whose creative abilities are brought into disrepute by distasteful alteration. They are principally concerned with protecting the reputation of the artist or author.

There are four kinds of moral right. First there is *the right to be identified as the author* of a work. Secondly, there *is the right to object to derogatory treatment* of a work. Thirdly, there is the *right not to have works falsely attributed to you*. Finally, and in a slightly different class, there is a *right to privacy of certain kinds of photographs* and films.

Right to be identified as the author
This applies to literary, dramatic, musical or artistic works and films. There are certain exceptions, such as computer programs. It is sometimes called the "paternity right," probably also from the French (it may be thought that this is a physiologically and psychologically implausible term as well as being sexist).

An author (or director in the case of a film) has the right to be identified as such, broadly speaking, whenever the work in question is exposed to the public. So in the case of a literary work, for example, whenever the work is published commercially, the author can insist that his or her name appears as the author. Or in the case of a film, when, for example, it is shown in public, broadcast or included in a cable programme service, the director can insist that he or she is credited. Architects can insist that they are identified on the buildings they have designed.

But before anyone can insist on such identification they have to assert their right. This can be done in various ways—either by a simple written document, signed by the author or the director or upon an assignment of copyright (say when an author hands over the copyright in a manuscript to a publisher). Nowadays, one commonly sees at the beginning of books (see this one) a recognition of the assertion by the author of their rights to be identified as the author.

If the right is infringed, a person has the right to claim damages and an injunction.

Right to object to derogatory treatment

This is the most troublesome of the moral rights. The Copyright Designs and Patents Act 1988 says that a treatment is derogatory "if it amounts to distortion or mutilation of the work or is otherwise prejudicial to the honour or reputation of the author or director." Because this law is so new, there is no real guidance as to what this means. The florid terminology "honour or reputation" sounds like something out of another age and it will be interesting to see what the courts make of it. Suppose, for example, a book publisher crops a photograph to make it fit the page or colours in a black and white sketch, the better to appeal to popular taste. Is that derogatory? More importantly, who should have the final say as to what is derogatory? Is it the artist? Or should one look to what "ordinary members of the public" would think? Or the judge hearing the case? These are interesting problems for the future.

Since the law is intended to protect the reputation of the artist or author, it is not an infringement if the author or director is not identified or has not previously been identified with the work or if there is sufficient disclaimer. There is no general right to prevent mutilation—the right is mainly there to prevent people thinking that the artist was responsible for it. Also, for example, making an adaptation or arrangement cannot *per se* amount to derogatory treatment—it must actually affect the author's honour or reputation.

This moral right does not apply to works made for reporting current events or in relation to the publication in newspapers of works made for that purpose. Nor does it apply to works where copyright is owned by someone's employer (when the person has made the work in the course of her employment pursuant to a contract of service). There are some other exceptions.

As with the right to be identified as the author, the right to object to derogatory treatment is infringed, essentially, by people who put the mutilated or distorted work before the public. So, the right is infringed, for example, by someone who publishes commercially a derogatory treatment of a work or issues copies to the public. In the case of a film, it would be infringed by someone who showed the film in public, broadcast it or included it in a cable programme service.

The right to object to derogatory treatment is also infringed (essentially) by people who deal in works which have been subjected to derogatory treatment knowing or having reason to believe that they have been subjected to derogatory treatment.

There are certain other exceptions—for example, the BBC can chop works around with impunity in order "to avoid the inclusion in a programme broadcast by them of anything which offends against good taste or decency or which is likely to encourage or incite to crime or to lead to disorder or be offensive to public feeling."

False attribution of authorship

The law of defamation is there to prevent people saying untrue and unfortunate things about people. This law is there to prevent other people thinking that you have said or done damaging things. Few things are as likely to bring a reputable author into disrepute, as it being said "So and so wrote X" where X is some especially unmeritorious work. This right gives a person the right not to have a literary, dramatic, musical or artistic work falsely attributed to him or her as author. It gives a similar right to directors, in relation to films.

Again, it is an infringement to put a work before the public in or on which there is a false attribution (for example, by exhibiting it if it is an artistic work or by issuing copies to the public, if it is a literary work). It is also infringed by someone who deals in works on which there is a false attribution knowing or having reason to believe that there is an attribution thereon and it is false. There are various other restricted acts.

The right does not only protect authors and directors. It is potentially valuable in the hands of interviewees of newspapers.

Example:
In 1969, the News of the World published an article with the headline "How My Love For The Saint Went Sour By Dorothy Squires talking to Weston Taylor." (The Saint was a well known TV series with the main hero played by Roger Moore.) Dorothy Squires sued for libel and for false attribution of authorship. The jury awarded her £4,300 for the libel and an extra £100 for false attribution of authorship. The Court of Appeal agreed. Lord Denning said, with characteristic pithiness "The article purports to be written by Dorothy Squires. It says 'By Dorothy Squires.' That was untrue. She did not write it." So she won.

Right to privacy of certain photographs and films

If, *for private and domestic purposes*, a person commissions a photograph or the making of a film, if copyright subsists in the resulting work, he or she has the right not to have copies of it issued to the public, the work exhibited or shown in public or the work broadcast or included in a cable programme service. So wedding photographs should be safe from media exposure.

Duration of moral rights and waiver

Moral rights last so long as copyright subsists in the work except that the right to object to derogatory treatment lasts for 20 years after a person's death. They can be disposed of by will. A person can waive any of the moral right by an instrument signed in writing and people who commission works often insist that authors waive all their moral rights.

24

THE EUROPEAN COMMUNITY—FREE MOVEMENT AND COMPETITION

The influence of European Community law

European Community (EC) law has had a very great influence on intellectual property. Intellectual property rights are territorial (for example a United Kingdom patent only gives a person the right to prevent competitors dealing in the product in the United Kingdom). They are also "anti-competitive" (for example, a valid registered trade mark gives the proprietor the exclusive right to use the trade mark in the United Kingdom on the goods for which it is registered). A patent involves the State authorising a person to exclude competition.

EC law on the other hand points in the opposite direction—the EC Treaty is set against territorial rights and is pro-competition. It outlaws restrictions on the freedom of movement of goods across national boundaries and there are specific provisions directed against anti-competitive abuses of market power and restrictive agreements.

There are also United Kingdom laws which mitigate the anti-competitive effects of intellectual property but these are of lesser importance in practice than European Community law.

How are these two approaches to be reconciled?

FREE MOVEMENT—ARTICLES 30 AND 36

Articles 30 and 36 of the Treaty of Rome provide for the free movement of goods. Article 30 says that quantitative restrictions on imports and measures having equivalent effect are to be prohibited. But Article 36 allows for prohibitions or restrictions for the protection of industrial and commercial property provided that they are not a means of arbitrary discrimination or disguised restriction of trade between Member States.

The European Court of Justice has worked out special principles which aim to reconcile the free movement of goods with the territoriality of intellectual property rights.

The fundamental rules

First, although the Treaty does not affect the *existence* of an intellectual property right, there are circumstances in which its *exercise* can be prohibited. Second, Article 36 permits exceptions to the free movement of goods only to the extent to which those exceptions are necessary to safeguard the rights that constitute the *specific subject matter* of the type of intellectual property in question. Third, the right holder's rights are *exhausted* when the goods are put into circulation by her (or with her consent), anywhere within the Common Market.

As will be seen, these principles only give guidance at the most abstract level. The effect of them is best illustrated by a few examples.

Example 1 (patents):
Sterling Drug held patents for a urinary infection drug in both the United Kingdom and the Netherlands. They sold the drug cheaply in the United Kingdom but it was very expensive in the Netherlands. Centrafarm bought some of the drug in the United Kingdom and shipped it to the Netherlands. They sold it there at a handsome profit. Held: there was nothing that Sterling Drug could do about this. The rights were exhausted by putting the drug into circulation for the first time in the United Kingdom. (*Centrafarm* v. *Sterling Drug* 1974). (Note, the result would be the same if the patentee first sold into a country where there was no patent protection. Note also, there are special rules governing the manner in which repackaging of parallel imports must be undertaken.)

Example 2 (same with trade marks):
Metro bought "Polydor" marked records in France (where they were cheap) and sold them in Germany (where they were expensive). Held: there was nothing that the trade mark proprietor could do to stop this (*Deutsche Grammophon* v. *Metro*, 1971).

Comparative Example 3: (unconnected parties)
Terranova, who had the mark TERRANOVA registered in Germany, tried to prevent Terrapin (an unconnected company) from importing building materials into Germany bearing the TERRAPIN mark. Held: Terranova could do so, provided that the mark did not act as an arbitrary means of discrimination or a disguised restriction on trade between Member States (*Terrapin* v. *Terranova*, 1976).

COMPETITION—ARTICLES 85 AND 86

There are two important provisions of the Treaty dealing with competition, Article 85 and Article 86. They are designed to ensure that there is competition "sans frontiéres" in Europe so that in order to come within either article, it must be shown that the agreement or conduct complained in question has an "effect on trade between Members States" of the EC.

Article 85

This prohibits agreements which have as their object or effect the prevention, restriction or distortion of competition within the Common Market. It is of general application, although there are some specific examples given in the Article of agreements which would normally be caught such as price fixing, or market sharing agreements.

In the field of intellectual property, Community law is especially concerned about the following practices under Article 85: tying (for example, a patentee insisting that a licensee of a process purchase all raw materials for operating the process from the patentee); charging royalties on non-patented products; obliging a licensee to disclose all the new technical information he learns to the patentee.

English law has something to say about tying too. Under the Patents Act 1977, agreements which require a licensee or purchaser to buy non-patented material from the patentee or his nominee are void. As an additional disincentive to such agreements, while one is in force, a patentee cannot enforce his patent against anyone.

Block exemptions

In order to provide some measure of certainty and predictability, the EC has enacted Regulations which grant clearance to certain kinds of intellectual property agreement. These are very useful. If people tailor their agreements to fit the block exemptions they will normally be safe. Although an agreement which falls within one of the block exemption Regulations will ordinarily be regarded as satisfying the competition rules there are no complete guarantees.

In the field of intellectual property, there are block exemption Regulations dealing with patent licensing agreements, know-how licensing agreements, research and development agreements and franchising.

Article 86

Article 86 prohibits abuses of dominant position. Being in a dominant position consists of possessing significant market power and ordinarily it will be judged by the size of market share. A market share of greater than 40 per cent., with the other competitors having much smaller shares is one rule of thumb that is often used. There are often disputes over what the relevant market is. Possession of an intellectual property right (such as a patent) can put a person into a dominant position but does not necessarily do so. It depends on a range of factors such as whether there are competing products and the extent to which the proprietor of the patent can act independently of other competitors and consumers.

Whether a person is abusing a dominant position must be judged individually in each case. Examples of conduct which may constitute abuse are charging excessive prices for products protected by a patent or refusing to licence except upon restrictive terms.

ENFORCING THE EC COMPETITION RULES

The European Commission

The European Commission is the administrative institution of the EC. It is split into a number of Directorates General (commonly called "DGs"), each responsible for a particular area of law or policy. One of the most powerful DGs (DGIV) deals with competition policy. DGIV used to be headed by Sir Leon Brittan (one of the Commissioners), a pro-competition enthusiast. At the time of writing, the Commissioner responsible for Competition policy is Karel van Miert. It is too early to say what his regime will be like. DGIV is very important for those concerned with intellectual property. Under the competition rules of the Treaty, a person who is the victim of an anti-competitive agreement or an abuse of dominant position can make a complaint to the Commission. If there is a prima facie case, DGIV will open formal proceedings. A team of (mainly) lawyers and economists is assigned to the case and it conducts an investigation. There are extensive powers (mainly set out in so called "Regulation 17") to investigate and compel persons to produce documents. The Commission also investigates of its own initiative and can conduct "dawn raids" on companies throughout the Community, suspected of anti-competitive practices taking away incriminating documents.

If the Commission considers that there has been a violation of EC competition law, it sends the person concerned a "Statement of Objections." The person is entitled to an oral hearing and to put their case with witnesses.

Then, if the Commission finds that a person has infringed the competition provisions of the Treaty, it can order the person concerned to stop. It can also order the payment of fines of up to 10 per cent. of turnover of the undertaking concerned. Some recent fines have run into tens of millions of pounds.

In practice, a large number of cases are settled informally. The parties will agree (for example) to remove offending terms from an agreement and DGIV will send an informal letter confirming that they are no longer interested in the case.

One advantage for complainants before the Commission is that they do not have to pay their opponent's costs if they lose—unlike in the United Kingdom courts. The Commission takes charge of the proceedings and is primarily responsible for pursuing it. Fending off a Commission investigation can be a very costly and inconvenient business. So a threat of a complaint to the Commission is often enough to have some effect.

People who are worried that their conduct may contravene the Treaty can ask the Commission for a formal or informal exemption (comfort letter) in advance. This is in addition to the block exemptions, discussed above, which provide prima facie exemption from the Treaty provisions.

The European Courts

If the parties are dissatisfied with a Commission decision, they can appeal it to the Court of First Instance and ultimately to the European Court of Justice. The European Court of Justice is set against artificial barriers to trade and, on important matters, more often than not, upholds the Commission.

The United Kingdom Courts—"Euro-defences"

Defendants (especially defendants to patent and copyright cases) quite often raise so-called "Euro-defences." A Euro-defence is a claim that for the plaintiff to enforce his rights against the defendant would be contrary to the Treaty of Rome, especially Articles 85 or 86. For example, it is sometimes said that a patentee who has licensed his patent to others, is unjustly (and anti-competitively) discriminating against the defendant in refusing to licence the patent to him. Or it is said that a copyright owner is using the copyright to obtain an unjust monopoly in another field (see *Magill*, 1991—TV companies trying to enforce copyright in TV listings).

Euro-defences are rarely successful. In order to be able to rely on one, a defendant has to show that there is some nexus between the intellectual property right asserted and the alleged abuse. A defendant also has to show that there is an effect on trade between Member States. It is usually rather difficult to do this and Euro-defences are often struck out before they get a chance to go to trial because there is no real prospect of the defendant showing either.

It is commonly said among intellectual property practitioners that Euro-defences are the last defence of the pirate. The courts certainly look on them with some scepticism. Although acknowledging that some such defences have merit, the dominant view is: "Whatever else it is, the Treaty of Rome is not intended to be a pirate's charter" (*British Leyland* v. *T.I.*, 1979).

EC law gives rights of action

As well as providing potential defences, European competition law can provide a basis for actions in the United Kingdom courts. Articles 85 and 86 are "directly effective" in the courts and a person who has infringed them may be liable to pay damages. They may also be stopped by injunction (including an interlocutory injunction, in a suitable case). The Commission, overburdened with work, and seeking to give effect to a principle of subsidiarity has been encouraging national courts to apply the competition provisions, rather than leaving it to the Commission to pursue complaints. Litigation in this area is a growing field.

One of the main differences between EC and United Kingdom competition law, is that the EC law gives a much greater role to persons injured by anti-competitive practices to take action in the courts to put a stop to them and claim damages. Also, before being able to take action under EC law, a person must show that the conduct complained of has an effect on trade between Member States. However, the government is seriously considering introducing legislation very similar to Articles 85 and 86 to deal with purely domestic competition matters.

EC legislation

By 1776 copyright and patents were sufficiently important commercially to warrant mention in the United States Constitution as something which the *federal* Congress could legislate about (Art. 1, s.

8 (8)). Over the years intellectual property has become more and more of an international matter and in the EC too it is getting to be a "federal" question rather than a Member States' question.

We have seen the obstacles which intellectual property rights place in the way of free movement of goods and services, but there is nothing specifically about the EC's power to regulate intellectual property in the Treaty of Rome. That has not stopped the legislative programme. As part of the move to create a single market, the EC has passed a fair amount of legislation in the field of intellectual property which is intended to harmonise legislation between Member States. For example, there are now directives on the harmonisation of trade mark law in the Member States, on video rental rights and on computer software copyright.

EC directives set out in fairly general terms what the Member States have to introduce by way of legislation but give Member States some leeway in how that is to be done. A deadline is set for passing suitable legislation and Member States have to introduce something which complies by the deadline. What happens if the United Kingdom fails to introduce conforming legislation by the deadline? If the provisions of the directive are precise and unconditional, a person can rely on these provisions against administrative authorities of the state (and certain other organs of the state, but not against other private citizens), even though there is no national legislation implementing the directive. This is the doctrine of "direct effect" developed by the European Court of Justice over 20 years ago as an instance of the supremacy of EC law.

The direct effect doctrine may have important implications in the field of trade mark law. The EC trade mark harmonisation directive has not yet been implemented by the United Kingdom. But the deadline for implementation (January 1, 1993) has passed. People should therefore be entitled to rely on the provisions of the directive against the Registrar of Trade Marks (an organ of the State) so long as there is no national legislation clearly contrary to the directive (*Marleasing*, 1990). It may also be possible, at least in theory, to claim damages against the state for failure to implement the directive.

25

SOME INTERNATIONAL ASPECTS OF INTELLECTUAL PROPERTY LAW

We will just look at two aspects of international intellectual property law, a topic of ever increasing importance.

Foreign intellectual property rights

Issues of the subsistence of a intellectual property right can usually only be decided in the courts of the country whose laws confer the right and the courts of other countries have no right to judge these. This is best illustrated by two examples.

Example 1:

In 1984 a company called Tyburn Productions produced a television film called "The Masks of Death" from a script original in every respect except that it featured Sherlock Holmes and Dr. Watson. It tried to distribute the film in the United States and received an angry letter from the only surviving child of Sir Arthur Conan Doyle, a Lady Jean Bromet. She claimed copyright in the characters her father had created. Tyburn appeased her by the payment of a substantial sum of money and an undertaking to delay distribution.

Some time later Tyburn wanted to produce another film—"The Abbott's Cry"—again an original script but also based on the Sherlock Holmes character. Making the film would involve them in substantial production costs and they wanted to be sure that they could distribute it in the United States before incurring too much expense. A mere assertion by Lady Bromet of her copyright would have seriously affected distribution. So they tried to clear the matter up in advance. It was not possible to force Lady Bromet to sue them so that their rights could be tested. Nor could they sue for a declaration in the United States. So they tried to enlist the help of the English courts. The court held that the question whether Lady Bromet was entitled to copyright under United States law was not something an English court could decide. It was not justiciable in England. (*Tyburn Productions* v. *Doyle*, 1990.)

Example 2:

For many years an ancient order of clever Carthusian monks brewed a delicious liqueur at the monastery of La Grande Chartreuse in France. The liqueur was brewed according to a secret process, jealously guarded. As well as being enormously devout, the monks were evidently shrewd businessmen, and the head of the order, the procurator, one Abbè Rey, ensured that "Chartreuse" trade marks were registered in various countries, including France and the United Kingdom.

Tragedy befell the order when, in 1901, the French Government passed a law which declared illegal all unlicensed religious associations failing to obtain authorisation from the State. The monks applied for authorisation, but the French Government (which probably thought the Carthusians had had it too good for too long) refused and the order was dissolved. The monks were forcibly expelled from France and all their property, including their trade marks, was confiscated and sold. But one thing not even the French Government could take away from them was their secret process. That the monks carried with them into their Spanish exile where, not too far from the French border, they cocked a snook at the French Government, and set up in business again. The monks were as devout as ever and the liqueur was as delicious as ever.

The inevitable happened. The liquidator, Monsieur Lecouturier, purported to grant the right to sell Chartreuse liqueur to another (who did not have the secret). Trade mark war broke out. The monks sought to prevent the liquidator, and those claiming under him, from importing liqueur marked "Chartreuse" into England, relying on their English trade marks. At first, they succeeded. But then the liquidator "by a contrivance which it is difficult to reconcile with the actual truth" (as the House of Lords charitably put it) somehow got the English trade marks transferred to him, alleging that he was the assignee of the Abbè Rey. The liquidator then tried the reverse trick and managed to prevent the monks from importing their Chartreuse into England.

The House of Lords was evidently outraged. Lord Shaw said: "I do not see anything conferring upon the liquidator of the property of the Carthusian Order a right to strip that order of their possessions in all parts of the world." It was held that the property in question (the English trade mark) was situated in England and must therefore be regulated according to the laws of England. The French transfer did not confer title to the English marks on the liquidator and the monks won. (*Rey* v. *Lecouturier*, 1910.)

It is a matter of some dispute at present whether it is possible to sue someone in a different country for *infringement* of a European intellectual property right under the Brussels Convention. Prima facie, the convention confers such a right but if an attack is made on the *validity* or *subsistence* of the right, that must be made in the courts of the State conferring the right.

Of course one cannot sue in any country for infringement if no acts have been done in the jurisdiction of the country conferring the right which constitute infringement. So, for example, one cannot sue for infringement of an English trade mark in respect of any acts done in Ireland.

Foreigners generally entitled to claim United Kingdom intellectual property rights

Most foreigners are entitled to many of the copyrights in the United Kingdom pursuant to various mutual recognition treaties such as the Berne Convention. United Kingdom copyright legislation makes special provision for people who are not British citizens to qualify for United Kingdom copyright protection. The rules governing foreigners' rights to claim particular kinds of copyright (such as copyright in films) can be very complicated and reference should always be made to more detailed works and the statutory materials.

The position with design right is less generous to foreigners: for example, although United States citizens can claim United Kingdom copyright, they are not, at least not yet, entitled to (unregistered) design right. The United States is a rather special case as regards mutual recognition of intellectual property rights but it is slowly falling into line.

Any foreigner or foreign company can apply for a United Kingdom trade mark, patent or registered design and can sue for passing-off (if there is a reputation in the United Kingdom). For example, the famous Parisian restaurant, Maxim's, could maintain an action for passing-off against a restaurant, in Norwich, decorated in French period style and called "Maxim's" (*Maxim's* v. *Dye*, 1977.)

Foreign plaintiffs are treated exactly the same way as domestic plaintiffs in litigation but they sometimes have to provide security for the costs of litigation where domestic plaintiffs do not.

There are several multilateral treaties which provide for mutual grant of intellectual property rights in different countries. The most important are the Berne and Paris Conventions.

26

MISCELLANEA, FUTURE DEVELOPMENTS AND FURTHER READING

SPECIAL RIGHTS

In addition to the important series of rights described in the foregoing chapters there are other rather specialised rights, akin to copyright, patents or trade marks, dealing with special problems. We have seen one instance in the shape of certification trade marks. Here are some others.

Plant breeder's rights

Plant breeder's rights work a bit like patents but the procedure for obtaining them is separate from the patents system. The Plant Varieties and Seeds Act 1964 is the basic legislation and there is a special Plant Varieties Office.

For a variety to be protected it must be new, distinct, uniform and stable. By "new" is meant "not previously commercialised." The Plant Varieties Office (presided over by a Controller) examines applications for plant variety rights, and will only allow them to be granted in respect of those varieties for which a special scheme has been made for the relevant genus or species to which the variety belongs. There are different periods of protection for different species (ranging from 15 to 25 years).

The plant variety right only extends to marketing of reproductive material (*e.g.* seeds, cuttings or, as in a recent case, turf—*Germinal v. Fell*, 1992) and there are express provisions for farmers to make their own seed from their own crop and compulsory licensing to prevent abuses of monopoly. There are also special provisions governing the names of new varieties.

Performers' rights and recording rights

Bootlegging has long been a problem in the entertainment business. Until the Copyright, Designs and Patents Act 1988 there was a kind of legal fudge which gave performers some rights to prevent these. There were also criminal provisions. However, the effect of the fudge was to give performers rights that were too extensive and to give recording companies (who cared most about bootlegging) no real rights at all. This is what the 1988 Act tried to sort out.

In essence, the new law gives a performer a right to control the exploitation of his or her performances. It also gives a person with exclusive recording rights in connection with such a performance the right to prevent exploitation of illicit recordings (either by dealing in copies of them or by broadcasting the performance). Various criminal offences are also created.

There are certain qualifying requirements (mainly nationality or residence of the performer or the place where the performance took place). These are very liberal and the likelihood is that if the person performing could get an English copyright, he or she would be entitled to a performers' right as well.

As regards recording rights, in order to be entitled to these, a person must have an exclusive recording contract (*i.e.* a contract entitling that person, to the exclusion of all other persons including the performer, to make recordings with a view to their commercial exploitation). Similar rights to performers' rights are given—essentially to prevent exploiting illicit recordings.

Performers' rights and recording rights subsist for 50 years from the year in which the performance took place.

Rental rights

This is a right which arises under the Copyright Designs and Patents Act 1988 although it is a bit different from the other copyrights. A copyright owner is, in essence, given the right to take a reasonable royalty every time a sound recording (tape, record or CD), film (including video film) or computer program is rented to the public. This is of considerable commercial importance and, to avoid abuse of monopoly, the Copyright Tribunal can set an appropriate royalty.

Public lending right

Similar to the rental right, the public lending right gives authors a right to claim a royalty every time one of their books is borrowed from a public library. The book must be registered under an appropriate scheme and the author can claim royalties which are calculated according to a complex formula, taking into account the average number of times the book is lent out. Payment is made out of central funds.

FUTURE DEVELOPMENTS

One of the most prolific sources of new intellectual property law at the moment is the European Community. In the field of patents the most important area of activity is in the legal protection of biotechnological inventions, following the debates at the European Patent Office about the approach to patentability of living matter. There are also proposals for an EC regulation on plant varieties. This is a major issue of public interest, environmental as well as commercial grounds. For example, there was much controversy when a patent was allowed for a mouse genetically engineered to develop cancer (*Oncomouse*, 1991) although this patent is currently under opposition. An opposition brought by Greenpeace challenging a patent for a herbicide resistant plant was recently decided in favour of the patentee.

On the copyright front, there are proposals for legislation harmonising the term of copyright in Member States and for protection of databases. There is also a substantial programme afoot to harmonise industrial design protection throughout the Community. At present there is a patchwork of rather dissimilar laws in different Member States.

There has been steady activity concerning trade marks. There are current proposals for a directive on comparative advertising and now and again some minor progress is made towards establishing a Community-wide trade mark system. No-one except the Community institutions appears to have a great deal of enthusiasm for this.

In the United Kingdom all is quiet on the legislative front as we write. However, some time in the near future, the Government will have to find time to enact a new Trade Marks Act to comply with the harmonisation directive.

NOTE: FURTHER READING

For those who are interested, we recommend some other books and materials which deal with these matters in greater depth.

Copyright, designs, patents and confidential information
Finding a good general book on the full range of intellectual property which treats the matter in some depth is not too easy. The best available now is Cornish, *Intellectual Property* (2nd ed., Sweet & Maxwell, 1989). It is not too expensive and there is a helpful companion book of materials to go with it.

One of the great legal texts (on any subject) is Laddie, Prescott & Vitoria, *The Modern Law of Copyright* (Butterworths, 1980). It is now out of date, but a new edition is promised any day which will be even better and is probably worth waiting for. For those who must have a comprehensive guide without delay, there is Copinger & Skone James *On Copyright* (13th ed., Sweet & Maxwell, 1991). Copinger is competent but expensive (£160). There are several other books available which contain the text of the 1988 Act in the back, together with a gloss on the text of the Act in the front (see for example those by Dworkin & Taylor, and Gavin McFarlane). They are worth a look but some may think that better value is to obtained by just buying the 1988 Act itself.

Kerly's *Law of Trade Marks and Trade Names* (12th ed., Sweet & Maxwell, 1986) is a most comprehensive guide to both trade marks and passing-off. There is no real rival to Kerly but Wadlow, *The Law of Passing-Off* (Sweet & Maxwell, 1990), is also comprehensive in coverage and up-to-date. The section on passing-off in *Halsbury* is particularly good.

As to patents, the standard work is Terrell, *On The Law of Patents* (Sweet & Maxwell, 1982). This cannot be described as a racy read. It is an ageing practitioners' guide, well regarded by the courts.

On a slightly different subject, but with some interesting chapters on intellectual property is Robertson & Nicol, *Media Law* (2nd ed., Longman, 1990).

EEC law and competition

All the main intellectual property text books have a chapter or two on intellectual property and EC law. The one in Kerly's *Law of Trade Marks and Trade Names* (12th ed., Sweet & Maxwell, 1986) is very good.

For a general introduction to EC law see *Wyatt and Dashwood's European Community Law* (3rd ed., Sweet & Maxwell, 1993)—gives a good overview—well written.

For good accounts of EC competition law see Korah, *An Introductory Guide to EEC Competition Law and Practice* (4th ed., ESC Publishing, 1990)—very readable and interesting account, short; and Bellamy and Child, *Common Market Law of Competition* (3rd ed., Sweet & Maxwell, 1987) (4th ed. Autumn 1993)—competent practitioner's work but not a relaxing read.

For both United Kingdom and EC competition law see Whish, *Competition Law* (2nd ed., Butterworths, 1989)—good but fat.

INDEX